How to Become a United States Citizen

A Step-by-Step Guidebook for Self-Instruction

Sixth Edition

Como Hacerse Ciudadano de los Estados Unidos

Una Guía Detallada de Auto-Instrucción

Sexto Edición

by Sally A. Navarro
Teacher (and daughter of immigrant parents)

Nolo Press Occidental
2425 Porter Street #19, Soquel, CA 95073
831 479-1520

Printing History

First edition: July 1983
    Second printing: October 1984

Second edition: August 1986

Third edition: January 1988
    Second printing: June 1988
    Third printing: October 1988
    Fourth printing: April 1989

Fourth edition: January 1992
    Second printing: August 1992

Fifth edition: June 1995
    Second printing: January 1996

Sixth edition: July 2002

Assistant to the author: Randall J. Navarro

Spanish translation: Jacquelyn Kole Gillespie

Cover design: Ben Thompson

Book design: Stephen Pollard

ISBN: 0-944508-39-1

Library of Congress Control Number: 2001091838

Dedication

This book is dedicated to my "daddy," Johannes Wilhelmus Brand, who in 1923 at age twenty immigrated to the United States from the Netherlands on a ship called the *New Amsterdam.* Tears of joy streamed down his face, he told me, when he first laid eyes on the Statue of Liberty, the symbol of this land of opportunity, land of the free, and place for the American dream to become a reality. Dad immediately found work, studied English at night school, then married my mother, Anna Johanna Stoof. He provided well for our family (of five daughters) with hard work and long hours. Dad lived the American dream and knew he was living it when he said, "Sally, this is the best country in the world!" I believed him. And it was his example that became the inspiration for this book. May you, like my dad, enrich America and fully enjoy the experience America offers through United States citizenship!

Acknowledgments

We are deeply indebted to Dan P. Danilov Esq., one of the country's most prominent immigration attorneys, for his valuable suggestions and enthusiastic support from early on — beginning with the first edition (1983) to this, the sixth. Mr. Danilov has practiced immigration law exclusively for over 40 years and has authored many publications, among them the book *Immigrating to the U.S.A.* Time taken from his very busy professional life in Seattle, Washington, to help with this book was an act of real generosity for which we are truly grateful.

A very special gratitude is extended to my son, Randall J. Navarro, whose countless hours and endless patience in assisting me every step of the way truly made this sixth edition possible. Thanks, *mi hijo!* Your grandpa would be proud.

Appreciation also goes to my husband, Fred Navarro, for making do so well during all the time that I was focused solely on this project. Thanks also to Tony Sisca, our friend, for so graciously lending his expertise as historical consultant.

Contenido

Contents

Apéndices

Formularios ejemplares

Introducción

El objetivo de este libro es ayudarle a usted mismo con el procedimiento entero de hacerse ciudadano de los Estados Unidos. Ya que este es un libro de auto-ayuda completo, usted se puede preparar para la ciudadanía en la conveniencia y la comodidad de su hogar, cuando usted tenga el tiempo disponible y a su propio paso. Se proporcionan para usted ejemplares de los formularios ya completados. También le familiarizarán con qué esperar mientras pasa usted por el procedimiento de hacerse ciudadano de los Estados Unidos.

El procedimiento de la naturalización, comenzando con la solicitud y terminando con el juramento de fidelidad, puede tomar hasta 6 a 12 meses o más. Debido a la duración de tiempo que toma, usted puede decidir comenzar el procedimento de la naturalizacion por entregar una solicitud inmediatamente cuando usted sea calificado. ¡Entre más pronto comience, más pronto se hará usted ciudadano de los EE.UU!

Nota

La intención de este libro es proveer información precisa y autorizada con respecto al procedimiento de la naturalización para la ciudadanía estadounidensa. Todo cuidado se ha tomado en la escritura de él, y se han consultado a los individuos necesarios y las materias de referencia apropiadas, especialmente ésos del Servicio de Inmigración y Naturalización del Ministerio de Justicia de los Estados Unidos. Sin embargo, las leyes federales tocante a la naturalización pueden cambiar. Así es que, para información más detallada o actualizada, especialmente en los casos complejos, el solicitante debe consultar al Servicio de Inmigración y Naturalización o a un abogado de inmigración.

Introduction

The aim of this book is to help you through the entire process of becoming a United States citizen. Because this is a complete self-help book, you can prepare for citizenship in the convenience and comfort of your home, at your leisure, and at your own pace. Forms are already filled out to provide examples for you. They will also familiarize you with what to expect as you make your way through the process of becoming a United States citizen.

The naturalization process, beginning with filing an application and ending with your taking an oath of allegiance, may take 6 to 12 months or more. Because of the length of time it takes, you may decide to begin the process of naturalization by filing an application immediately when you become qualified. The sooner you start, the sooner you become a U.S. citizen!

Note

This book is intended to provide accurate and authoritative information regarding the process of naturalization for United States citizenship. Every care has been taken in the writing of it, and appropriate individuals and reference materials have been consulted, especially those from the Immigration and Naturalization Service of the United States Department of Justice. However, federal laws regarding naturalization are subject to change. Therefore, for more detailed or updated information, particularly in complex cases, the applicant should consult the Immigration and Naturalization Service or an immigration attorney.

Capítulo Uno
Todo lo Referente a la Naturalización

¿Qué es la naturalización?

Sencillamente, "la naturalización" quiere decir el proceso en que un inmigrante se haga ciudadano. El Congreso ha aprobado leyes de la naturalización que exponen las condiciones bajo los cuales los inmigrantes se puedan hacer ciudadanos. Tales leyes intentan que un inmigrante pueda hacerse ciudadano solamente si él o ella, está dispuesto a aceptar los deberes y las responsabilidades de la ciudadanía y a conservar y proteger la democracia americana. Las leyes son iguales para los hombres y las mujeres de toda raza. Todos se vuelven ciudadanos al seguir el mismo proceso. Este libro es para orientarlo en tal proceso.

¿Cuáles son los beneficios de la naturalización?

¿Por qué hacerse ciudadano de los Estados Unidos? Sin duda, usted tiene buenas razones personales que lo hacen querer ser un ciudadano de los Estados Unidos. Pero, cualesquiera que sean, además de tener usted sus razones personales, es buena idea darse cuenta de los muchos e importantes beneficios de la naturalización, o ciudadanía estadounidensa:

- Usted va a poder votar en todas las elecciones.

- Usted calificará para los trabajos que requieren la ciudadanía estadounidensa.

- Usted les facilitará la inmigración a los Estados Unidos para sus parientes inmediatos que todavía vivan en el extranjero.

- Usted ya no tendrá que cargar su tarjeta permanente de residencia o sea "la mica," ni tendrá que notificarle al Servicio de la Inmigración y de la Naturalización de su dirección.

- Usted podrá obtener un pasaporte que indica que es ciudadano de los Estados Unidos — dándole la oportunidad de viajar afuera del país. También, usted recibe la protección y asistencia del gobierno estadounidense cuando viaja en el extranjero.

Chapter One
All About Naturalization

What is naturalization?

Simply, "naturalization" means the process by which an immigrant becomes a United States citizen. Congress has passed naturalization laws that set forth the conditions under which immigrants can become citizens. Such laws intend that an immigrant may become a citizen only if he or she is willing to accept the duties and responsibilities of citizenship and to preserve and protect American democracy. The laws are the same for men and women of all races. All become citizens by following the same procedure. This book is intended to help guide you through those procedures.

What are the benefits of naturalization?

Why become a United States citizen? You undoubtedly have good personal reasons prompting your desire to become a citizen of the United States. But in addition to your personal reasons, whatever they may be, it is a good idea to be aware of the many important benefits of naturalization, or United States citizenship:

- You will be able to vote in all elections.
- You will qualify for jobs that require United States citizenship.
- You will make immigration to the United States easier for your immediate relatives who still live abroad.
- You will no longer have to carry your Permanent Resident Card or notify the Immigration and Naturalization Service of your address.
- You will be able to obtain a passport indicating your United States citizenship — providing the freedom to travel outside the country. In addition, citizens receive U.S. Government protection and assistance when abroad.
- You can even run for public office, except those of President or Vice-President of the United States.

It is a nice feeling to know that as a citizen you, too, can fully share in this country's freedoms, with *all* the benefits and responsibilities that citizenship entails.

- Usted hasta podrá postularse para un puesto público con excepción a la presidencia o vice-presidencia de los EE.UU.

Es agradable saber que como un ciudadano, usted, también, puede participar completamente en las libertades del país, con *todos* los beneficios y responsabilidades que lleva al cabo la ciudadanía.

¿Quién se puede naturalizar?

Las personas como usted que inmigran legalmente a los Estados Unidos, que deciden hacerse ciudadanos, y que pasan por el proceso de la naturalización. Luego, usted puede disfrutar de los beneficios completos de la ciudadanía junto con esos ciudadanos que nacieron en los Estados Unidos.

Muchos millones de personas antes de usted, de todas partes del mundo y de todas nacionalidades, credos y colores, han llegado a los Estados Unidos para vivir. Debido a eso, no es extraño que la expresión "caldero de razas" se desarrolló. La Tabla 1 muestra de qué paises han originado una gran cantidad de inmigrantes. Las razones personales de esta multitud que vino a radicar a los Estados Unidos y que hicieron ciudadanos, probablemente fueron tan variadas como las personas mismas. Sólo se puede suponer que todos los inmigrantes esperan mejorar su estándar de vivir en los Estados Unidos, considerado por muchos como "la tierra de la oportunidad."

Tabla 1: Los 5 Paises con la Mayoría de los Inmigrantes	
1. México	4. India
2. Vietnam	5. China
3. Filipinas	

Información del Servicio de Inmigración y Naturalización

El Servicio de Inmigración y Naturalización

Se administran las solicitudes de la naturalización en el Departamento de Justicia, Inmigración, y Naturalización de los Estados Unidos, más conocido como el "INS." En 1998, el INS inauguró su "Modelo para el Nuevo Proceso de la Naturalización," un plan en que se realizaron grandes cambios en el program de ciudadanía, por un período de varios años. El programa nuevo fue desarrollado para mejorar la integridad del proceso de la naturalización, igual que mejorar el servicio del cliente estandarizando y automatizando los procedimientos por toda la nación. Como resultado, el INS aumentó el número de empleados, amplió sus facilidades, y renovó los procedimientos.

Who becomes naturalized?

People like you who legally immigrate to the United States, who choose to become citizens, and who go through the naturalization process. You may then enjoy the full benefits of citizenship right along with those citizens who were born in the United States.

Many millions of people before you, from all over the world and of all nationalities, creeds and colors, have come to the United States to live. Because of this, it is no wonder that the expression "melting pot" evolved. Table 1 shows from what countries a large number of immigrants have originated. The personal reasons for these multitudes settling in the United States and becoming citizens were probably as varied as the people themselves. We can only assume that all immigrants hope to better their standard of living in the United States, regarded by many as the "land of opportunity."

> **Table 1: Top 5 Countries of Origin**
>
> 1. Mexico   4. India
> 2. Vietnam   5. China
> 3. Philippines
>
> Source: Immigration and Naturalization Service

The Immigration and Naturalization Service

Naturalization applications are administered by the U.S. Department of Justice, Immigration and Naturalization Service, commonly called the "INS." In 1998, the INS unveiled its "Blueprint for the New Naturalization Process," a plan to dramatically overhaul the citizenship program over a several-year period. The new program was developed to strengthen the integrity of the naturalization process, as well as improve customer service by standardizing and automating procedures nationwide. As a result, the INS has substantially increased its staff, expanded its facilities, and revamped its procedures. Reorganization was very much needed in order to handle the significant increase in naturalization applications which the INS began receiving in the mid-1990s as shown in Table 2. Processing time for naturalization applications varies among the different INS geographical regions, but it is the intention of the INS to nationally

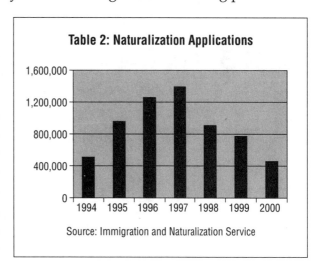

Table 2: Naturalization Applications

Source: Immigration and Naturalization Service

La reorganización fue muy necesaria, para tratar el aumento significativo en las solicitudes para la naturalización que el INS empezó a recibir al mediados de los años 1990's como se nota en la Tabla 2. El tiempo para procesar la solicitud de naturalización se varia entre las regiones geográficas del INS, pero el INS se intenta reducir el tiempo de espera por toda la nación hasta aproximadamente 6 meses. Entre-

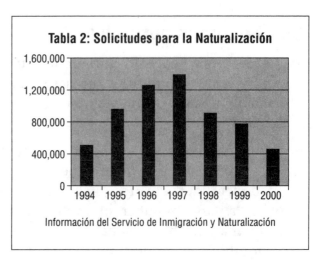

Tabla 2: Solicitudes para la Naturalización

Información del Servicio de Inmigración y Naturalización

tando, se recomienda que usted empiece el proceso de la naturalización, tan pronto como sea posible.

Una sobrevista del proceso de la naturalización

Las etapas siguientes resumen el proceso de la naturalización. Se describe cada etapa con detalles en los Capítulos Dos, Tres y Cuatro.

1. Preparando para solicitar

Primero, usted necesita confirmar su elegibilidad para la ciuda-danía, asegurándole que usted esté en conformidad con los requi-sitos de la naturalización enumerados al fin de este capítulo.

2. Llenando la solicitud

Llene la "Solicitud para la Naturalización", el Formulario N-400.

Saque *dos fotografías* que se conforman con los requisitos exactos del INS.

reduce the waiting time to approximately 6 months. Meanwhile, it is recommended you start the naturalization process as early as possible.

An overview of the naturalization process

The steps below summarize the process to naturalization. Details for each step are discussed in Chapters Two, Three and Four.

1. Preparing to apply

 First you need to confirm your eligibility for citizenship by ensuring you meet the naturalization requirements listed at the end of this chapter.

2. Completing your application

 Fill out your "Application for Naturalization," the Form N-400.

 Have *two photographs* taken which meet the exact INS requirements.

3. Getting fingerprinted

 Your fingerprints will be taken and sent to the U.S. Federal Bureau of Investigation for analysis on past criminal activity.

Fingerprints may be taken only at INS designated offices.

4. Filing your application for naturalization

 Mail the completed application, supporting documents, and appropriate fee(s) to the INS Service Center for your region. (See Appendix Five.)

3. Tomando las huellas dactilares

Se toman sus huellas dactilares y las envían al Departamento Federal de Investigaciones de los EE.UU. para el análisis de actividad criminal anterior.

Se toman las huellas dactilares solamente en las oficinas designadas del INS.

4. Someter la solicitud de naturalización

Envíe por correo la solicitud completada, los documentos adicionales, y el costo apropiado al Centro de Servicio del INS para su región. (Véase el Apéndice Cinco.)

5. La entrevista

El INS le enviará una carta de designación que especifica la hora y la localidad de su entrevista. Durante la entrevista, contestará preguntas sobre su pasado y su solicitud. También, tomará el examen de inglés y estudios cívicos seguido por una decisión sobre su "Solicitud para la Naturalización."

6. Tomar el juramento

¡El INS le notificará de la fecha y el lugar de la ceremonia en donde usted tomará el Juramento y finalmente recibirá el Certificado de la Naturalización! La ceremonia puede ocurrir en un tribunal o en un lugar menos formal. Los solicitantes normalmente pueden escoger el lugar que prefieren para tomar el Juramento.

Ponerse en contacto con el INS

La iniciativa reconstructiva de parte del INS, ha aumentado mucho las opciones disponibles al solicitante en cuanto a la comunicación con el INS. Además de hacer una visita en persona a la oficina del INS, se puede comunicarse con ellos por teléfono o computadora. Esto es un mejoramiento bienvenido, comparado con el pasado cuando era necesario hacer las visitas en persona a una oficina bien ocupada.

5. The interview

The INS will mail an appointment letter specifying the time and location for your interview. During your interview, you will answer questions about your application and background. In addition, you will take an English and civics exam followed by a decision on your "Application for Naturalization."

6. Taking the Oath

The INS will notify you of your ceremony date and location where you will take your Oath and finally receive a Certificate of Naturalization! The ceremony may take place in a courtroom or in a more casual setting. Applicants normally may choose which location they prefer to take the Oath.

Contacting the INS

The INS re-engineering initiative has greatly expanded the options an applicant has to communicate with the INS. In addition to making an in-person visit to the INS office, you may also make contact with the INS by phone or computer. This is a welcome improvement from the past, where an applicant normally had to make an in-person visit to an often crowded INS office.

Telephone: The INS has established two nationwide *toll-free* numbers to call and request naturalization forms, or talk directly with an INS official to obtain information, or ask questions and to inform the INS of your address change. The numbers are:

1-800-375-5283 (National Customer Service Center for *Information* and *Change of Address* notifications)

1-800-870-3676 (INS *Forms Requests* only)

At a minimum, you will need Form N-400, "Application for Naturalization." Better yet, consider ordering Form M-476, "A Guide to Naturalization," an informational packet (which includes the N-400).

Teléfono: El INS ha establecido dos números nacionales *sin tarifa o sea gratuito* en los cuales se puede pedir los formularios de naturalización, o hablar directamente con un funcionario del INS para obtener información, o hacer preguntas y para informar al INS de su cambio de dirección. Los números son:

1-800-375-5283 (Centro Nacional de Servicio para Clientes para *Información* y para notificación de *Cambios de Dirección.*)

1-800-870-3676 (*Pedir los formularios* del INS solamente.)

Al mínimo, se necesita el Formulario N-400, "Solicitud para la Naturalización." Más bien, considere pedir el Formulario M-476, "Un Guía a la Naturalización" un paquete informativo (que incluye el N-400) .

Computadora: Se puede obtener información sobre la naturalización y pedir formularios usando la computadora a través del sitio del Internet del INS ubicado en:

http://www.ins.usdoj.gov/graphics/formsfee/forms/n-400.htm

Oficinas del INS: Para los que desean presentarse en persona, el INS tiene Centros de Apoyo de la Solicitud (ASCs) para asistir a los solicitantes con el proceso de la naturalización.

Advertencia: Las oficinas del INS están muy ocupadas. Anticipe filas largas y una espera.

Los requisitos para la naturalización

Primero, usted debe de cumplir con ciertos requisitos que lo hacen elegible para hacerse ciudadano de los Estados Unidos por naturalización. En este momento, el INS tiene 7 requisitos que se pueden *variar* según las circunstancias individuales. Los requisitos son:

- Permanecer por cierto tiempo como residente permanente.

- Mantener residencia continua en los Estados Unidos.

Computer: Obtaining naturalization information and submitting forms requests may also be done by computer via the INS World Wide Web page located at:

http://www.ins.usdoj.gov/graphics/formsfee/forms/n-400.htm

INS Offices: For those desiring to visit in person, the INS has offices and Application Support Centers (ASCs) to assist applicants in the naturalization process.

Caution: INS offices tend to be very busy. Expect long lines and a wait.

The requirements for naturalization

You must first meet certain requirements in order to be eligible to become a U.S. citizen through naturalization. Currently, the INS has 7 naturalization requirements, which *vary* depending upon applicant's circumstances. These requirements are:

- Having a certain amount of time as a Permanent Resident.
- Having a continuous residence in the United States.
- Having a physical presence in the United States.
- Having the required time within an INS district or state.
- Having good moral character.
- Possessing adequate English and U.S. civics knowledge.
- Declaring an attachment to the U.S. Constitution.

The specific requirements vary for each applicant and are dependent on if you have any qualifying *special circumstance* that the INS recognizes for naturalization. These specific requirements are summarized in Table 3 on the following page.

Looking down, find the situation that best describes you. Looking across, see summary of your specific naturalization requirements.

Table 3 summarizes the requirements for approximately 90% of all eligible applicants. There are some less common circumstances, which may qualify an applicant for naturalization, or even for "speedy" U.S. citizenship for spouses of certain overseas U.S. workers. See *Appendix One* for more information.

- Tener una presencia física en los Estados Unidos.

- Pasar el tiempo requerido dentro de un distrito o estado del INS.

- Tener buena reputación moral.

- Conocer el inglés, la historia y el gobierno de los EE. UU. de modo suficiente.

- Declarar un enlace con la Constitución de los Estados Unidos.

Los requisitos específicos se varian entre cada solicitante, y son dependientes de si tenga usted alguna *circunstancia especial* calificativa que se reconozca el INS para la naturalización. Se los resumen estos requisitos específicos en la Tabla 3 de la página siguiente.

Los datos en la Tabla 3 se resumen los requisitos de aproximadamente 90% de todos los solicitantes elegibles. Hay circunstancias menos comunes por las cuales uno se pudiera calificar para la naturalización, o aún la ciudadanía "adelantada" de los EE.UU. para los esposos o las esposas de ciertos trabajadores estadounidenses de ultramar. Véase el *Apéndice Uno* para más información.

Repasamos ahora cada requisito para entender mejor lo que es necesario para llegar a ser ciudadano estadounidense.

Tiempo como Residente Permanente

Las leyes del momento de inmigración permiten que los inmigrantes lleguen a ser Residentes Permanentes (PR) de los Estados Unidos. A un inmigrante calificado se le concede el estado de "Residente Permanente" y se le da normalmente una Tarjeta de Residencia Permanente. (Anteriormente se llamaban las "Tarjetas del Registro Como Extranjero.") Un solicitante debe ser un residente permanente por una duración específica de años antes de solicitar la naturalización. Se permite hacer viajes afuera de los Estados Unidos mientras se acumula el tiempo de PR, pero hay que cuidarse de no poner en peligro otro requisito relacionado llamado la "residencia continua."

Residencia continua

La "residencia continua" mide la cantidad de tiempo en que usted estaba fuera de los Estados Unidos durante un *solo viaje*. Está en su mejor interés de guardar su tiempo al exterior menos de 6 meses. Si usted sale por un período de tiempo más largo, usted puede interrumpir el estado de su residencia continua. Los que estén en peligro de interrumpir su residencia continua generalmente caen en dos categorías:

REQUIREMENTS — Looking *down*, find the situation that best describes you. Looking *across*, see summary of your *specific* naturalization requirements	Time as a Permanent Resident (PR)	Continuous Residence	Physical Presence in the U.S.A.	Time in District or State	Good Moral Character	English and Civics Knowledge	Attachment to the Constitution
Have been a Permanent Resident for the past 5 years *and* have no special circumstances **Note: Most applicants fall into this category**	5 years	5 years as a Permanent Resident. Trips outside the U.S.A. for 6 months or longer are not permitted	30 months	3 months	Required	Required	Required
Have been continuously married to and living with a U.S. citizen for the past 3 years *and* your spouse has been a U.S. citizen during that period of time	3 years	3 years as a Permanent Resident. Trips outside the U.S.A for 6 months or longer are not permitted	18 months	3 months	Required	Required	Required
Are in the U.S. Armed Forces (or will be filing an application within 6 months of an honorable discharge) *and* have served at least 3 years	Just be a Permanent Resident on the day you file your application	Not Required	Not Required	Not Required	Required	Required	Required
Were in the U.S. Armed Forces for less than 3 years *or* were in the U.S. Armed Forces for 3 years or more, but you were discharged more than 6 months ago	5 years	5 years as a Permanent Resident. Trips outside the U.S.A for 6 months or longer are not permitted. **Note:** U.S. military service doesn't break your continuous residence	Not Required **Note:** U.S. military service abroad counts as time physically present in the U.S.A.	3 months	Required	Required	Required
Performed active duty military service in the U.S. Armed Forces during: • WW I (Nov. 11, 1916–Apr. 6, 1917) • WW II (Sep. 1, 1939–Dec. 31, 1946) • Korea (June 25, 1950–July 1, 1955) • Vietnam (Feb. 28, 1961–Oct. 15, 1978) • Persian Gulf (Aug. 2, 1990–Apr. 11, 1991)	No Permanent Resident time requirement **Note:** If you did not enlist or reenlist in the U.S. or its possessions, you must be a Permanent Resident on the day you file your application	Not Required	Not Required	Not Required	Required	Required	Required
Were married to *and* living with your U.S. citizen spouse who died during honorable active duty service in the U.S. Armed Forces	You must be a Permanent Resident on the day you file your application	Not Required	Not Required	Not Required	Required	Required	Required
Were married to *and* residing with certain U.S. citizen spouse who works overseas	Not Required "Speedy Naturalization"	Not Required	Not Required	Not Required	Required	Required	Required

Ausencias entre 6 a 12 meses: Se considera interrumpida la residencia continua si usted sale del país entre 6–12 meses *al menos* que usted pruebe que no. Para probar que *no* ha interrumpido el progreso de su residencia continua, necesitará someter el formulario 1722 del IRS, copia original, manifestando información sobre sus impuestos de los últimos 3 años. De otro modo, puede proveer copias de sus impuestos ya sometidos en los últimos 3 años. Es posible que el INS también se le exija algunos de los siguientes documentos:

- Prueba que su familia ha residido en los Estados Unidos durante su ausencia;

- Copias adicionales de sus impuestos;

- Copias de su pago de renta o de hipoteca; o

- Copias de su recibo de sueldo (talón de cheque).

Ausencias de 1 año o más: Normalmente, salir de los Estados Unidos por más de un año se le considera una interrumpción a su residencia continua. Al regresar, puede ser elegible entrar de vuelta como residente permanente *si* ha obtenido un permiso de volver a entrar. Pero sí será penalizado. El tiempo que usted acumuló *antes de que saliera* del país ya no cuente hacia su tiempo de la "residencia continua."

Sin embargo, si regresa a los Estados Unidos *dentro de 2 años*, el INS reconocerá algo de su tiempo afuera de los Estados Unidos. El INS cuenta los últimos 364 días *afuera* del país. Luego se puede contar y usar aquel tiempo para llenar el requisito para la residencia continua.

Hay algunos grupos de solicitantes que no tienen ningún requisito de residencia continua. (Como los miembros de Las Fuerzas Armadas de los EE.UU.) También, existen grupos más chicos que pueden salir del país por más de 1 año sin interrumpir su residencia continua. Las personas que caen en esta categoría deben iniciar una "Solicitud para Conservar la Residencia al Propósito de la Naturalización." (Formulario N-470), y obtener permiso *antes* de salir del país por más de un año. Comuníquese con el INS si tal vez se le aplique.

Presencia física en los Estados Unidos

La mayoría de los solicitantes deben estar físicamente presente en los Estados Unidos por un cierto número de meses para ser elegible para la naturalización. "La presencia física" es una medida de su tiempo adentro de los Estados Unidos. Los días pasados afuera de los Estados Unidos no cuentan como parte del requisito de la presencia física. Hay un pequeño número de solicitantes que pueden contar tiempo mientras que están afuera de los Estados Unidos hacia el requisito de la "presencia física." Por ejemplo, los miembros de las Fuerzas Armadas de los Esta-

Let's now review each of the requirements to gain a better understanding of what is required to become a U.S. citizen.

Time as a Permanent Resident

Current immigration laws allow immigrants to become Permanent Residents (PR) of the United States. A qualifying immigrant is granted "Permanent Resident" status and is normally given a Permanent Resident Card (previously called "Alien Registration" cards). Applicants must be a permanent resident for a specific number of years before applying for naturalization. Making trips outside the United States while accumulating PR time is allowed, but you must be careful to ensure a related requirement called "continuous residence" is not jeopardized.

Continuous residence

"Continuous residence" measures the amount of time you were outside the United States during a *single trip*. It is in your best interest to keep your time abroad to less than 6 months. If you leave for a longer period of time, you may interrupt your continuous residence status. Those in jeopardy of interrupting their continuous residence likely fall into two categories:

Absences between 6 and 12 months: Being outside of the United States for 6 to 12 months is considered a disruption of your continuous residence *unless* you can prove otherwise. To prove that you have *not* disrupted your continuous residence, you will need to submit an original IRS Form 1722 listing tax information for the past 3 years. Or, you may provide copies of the income tax forms you filed for the past 3 years. The INS may also ask that you provide any of the following:

- Proof that your family resided in the United States during your absence;
- Additional copies of tax records;
- Copies of rent or mortgage payments; or
- Copies of payroll stubs or statements.

Absences of 1 year or longer: Normally, leaving the United States for more than 1 year is considered a disruption of your continuous residence. Upon return, you may be eligible to re-enter as a permanent resident *if* you have a Re-entry permit. However, you will be penalized. None of the time you accumulated in the United States *before you left* the country will count toward your time in "continuous residence."

However, if you return to the United States *within 2 years*, the INS will recognize some of your time outside the United States. The INS will count the last 364 days of time outside of the country. This time can then be counted and used to meet your continuous residence requirement.

dos Unidos pueden incluir tiempo acumulado mientras que prestan servicio en el extranjero.

> **¡Importante!** Es importante comprender la *diferencia* entre la *residencia continua* y la *presencia física*. Incluso si usted nunca hiciera un viaje bastante largo para interrumpir su *residencia continua*, podría no reunir el requisito de la *presencia física* si hiciera varios viajes cortos del país.

Tiempo como residente en el distrito o estado

Se requiere a la mayoría de la gente vivir un mínimo de 3 meses en el distrito o el estado en que solicita la naturalización.

Buena reputación moral

Para ser elegible para la naturalización, un solicitante *debe* mostrar que tenga una buena reputación moral. El INS hará una determinación de su reputación moral basada en las respuestas que usted proporciona en su solicitud N-400 y en la entrevista. El INS se puede tomar en consideración lo siguiente en hacer determinación sobre la buena reputación moral.

Antecedentes criminales. Perpetrar algunos crímenes puede excluirle completamente de la naturalización. Se le revoca completamente su naturalización cuando exista alguna felonía agravada (perpetrada en o después del 29 de noviembre, 1990) o algún homicidio. Otros crímenes pueden causar una parada temporal, los cuales pueden prevenir el llegar a ser ciudadano por un período específico después de haber cometido el crimen.

Mentir. ¡Debe de decir la verdad! Si no, el INS puede negar su solicitud por falta de buena reputación moral. Se puede revocar la ciudadanía, si el INS se averigua que usted ha mentido en la solicitud o en la entrevista.

La "Solicitud para la Naturalización" (Formulario N-400) hace varias preguntas sobre crímenes. Debe de ser completamente *honesto* y revelar cualquier crimen que usted haya cometido. Sin embargo, no es necesario incluir violaciones menores de tránsito en la solicitud.

Ejemplos que pueden mostrar carencia de buena reputación moral:

- Cualquier crimen contra una persona con intención de hacerle daño.
- Cualquier crimen contra propiedades o el Gobierno que envuelva el fraude o intención malvada.
- Dos crímenes o más por los cuales la sentencia agregada era de 5 años o más.

There are a few groups of applicants who do not have any continuous residence requirement (such as members of the U.S. Armed Forces). There are also a few small groups who can leave the country for over 1 year and it will not disrupt their continuous residence. People who fall into this category must file an "Application to Preserve Residence for Naturalization Purposes" (Form N-470) and get it approved *before* being outside the country for over 1 year. Contact the INS if you think this may apply to your circumstance.

Physical presence in the United States

Most applicants are required to be physically present in the United States for a certain number of months in order to be eligible for naturalization. "Physical Presence" is a measure of your time inside the United States. Days spent outside the United States are not counted toward your physical presence requirement. There is a small number of applicants who may count time while outside the United States toward the "physical presence" requirement. For example, members in the U.S. Armed Forces may include time accumulated while serving overseas.

Important! It is important to understand the *difference* between *continuous residence* and *physical presence*. Even if you never took a trip long enough to disrupt your *continuous residence*, you might not meet the *physical presence* requirement if you took several short trips out of the country.

Time as a resident in district or state

Most people are required to live a minimum of 3 months in the district or state in which they are applying for naturalization.

Good moral character

To be eligible for naturalization, an applicant *must* be of good moral character. The INS will make a determination of your moral character based on the answers you provide in your N-400 application and during your interview. The INS may consider the following in making a good moral character determination:

Criminal record. Committing certain crimes could cause you to become totally ineligible for naturalization. Aggravated felonies (committed on or after November 29, 1990) and murder are considered permanent bars to naturalization. Other crimes may be grounds for a temporary bar, which would prevent you from becoming a citizen for a certain amount of time after you committed the crime.

Lying. You must tell the truth! If you do not, the INS may deny your application for lacking good moral character. Your citizenship could also be revoked if the INS

- Violar alguna ley de substancia controlada de los Estados Unidos, de cualquier estado o de un país extranjero.

- Ebrio habitual o manejar embriagado.

- Juego ilícito.

- Prostitución.

- Poligamia.

- Mentir para obtener algún beneficio para la inmigración.

- No hacer los pagos del hijo o de asistencia ordenados del tribunal.

- Encarcelación por 190 días o más en los últimos 5 años. (3 años si su solicitud está basada en el matrimonio a un ciudadano estadounidense.)

- Falta de completar un período probatorio, liberación condicional, o sentencia suspendida antes de solicitar para la naturalización.

- Si recientemente le han ordenado la deportación o la remoción.

- Actos del terrorista.

- Persecución de cualquier persona por causa de raza, religión, origen nacional, opinión político, o grupo social.

- Descargo o deserción de las Fuerzas Armadas de los Estados Unidos.

> **¡Importante!** Si usted ha cometido ciertos crímenes serios, el INS puede decidir removerle de los Estados Unidos. Se le recomienda *en sumo grado* que pida el consejo de un abogado de inmigración o de una organización de asistencia *antes de* solicitar la naturalización.

Requisitos para inglés y estudios cívicos

Según la ley, los solicitantes para la naturalización deben mostrar un nivel proficiente del inglés y un conocimento de los estudios cívicos o sea la historia y el gobierno.

- **Inglés:** Conocer el idioma inglés, incluso la habilidad de leer, escribir y hablar. El solicitante debe poder comunicarse con palabras y frases sencillas, lo que se considera un uso común del idioma inglés.

y

- **Estudios Cívicos:** Un conocimiento y entendimiento de los hechos fundamentales históricos y los principios y estructura del gobierno de los Estados Unidos.

were to later find out that you lied on your application or during your interview.

The "Application for Naturalization" (Form N-400) asks several questions about crimes. You should be completely *honest* and report any crime(s) that you may have committed. However, it is not necessary to include minor traffic violations on your application.

Examples that may show lack of good moral character:

- Any crime committed against a person with intent to harm.
- Any crime committed against property or the Government that involves fraud or evil intent.
- Two or more crimes for which the aggregated sentence was 5 years or more.
- Violating any controlled substance law of the United States, any state, or any foreign country.
- Habitual drunkenness or drunk driving.
- Illegal gambling.
- Prostitution.
- Polygamy.
- Lying to gain immigration benefits.
- Not paying court-ordered child support or alimony payments.
- Confinement in jail/prison for which the total confinement was 190 days or more during the past 5 years (3 years if you are applying based on marriage to a United States citizen).
- Failing to complete any probation, parole, or suspended sentence before you apply for naturalization.
- If you have recently been ordered deported or removed.
- Terrorist acts.
- Persecution of anyone because of race, religion, national origin, political opinion, or social group.
- Discharge or desertion from the U.S Armed Forces.

Important! If you have committed certain serious crimes, the INS may decide to remove you from the United States. It is *highly recommended* you seek advice from an immigration attorney or assistance organization *before* applying for naturalization.

Hay *excepciones* a estos requisitos para ciertos solicitantes debido a la edad, o a la incapacidad, cuales son:

Edad: Para el examen de inglés y los estudios cívicos, existen las siguientes excepciones basadas en la edad del solicitante al iniciar la solicitud.

- Ninguna prueba inglesa si usted tiene *más de 50* años y ha vivido dentro de los Estados Unidos como Residente Permanente por un período total de 20 años a lo menos. Tiene que tomar la prueba de estudios cívicos pero puede tomarla en el idioma de su preferencia.

- Ninguna prueba inglesa si usted tiene *más de 55* años y ha vivido en los Estados Unidos como Residente Permanente por un período total de 15 años a lo menos. Tiene que tomar la prueba de estudios cívicos pero puede tomarla en el idioma de su preferencia.

- Ninguna prueba inglesa si tiene *más de 65* años y ha vivivo en los Estados Unidos como Residente Permanente por un período total de 20 años a lo menos. Tiene que tomar la prueba de estudios cívicos pero puede tomarla en el idioma de su preferencia. Se puede tomar una versión más sencilla también.

Debe de reunir con estos requisitos cuando inicia su solicitud. Para calificarse para una excepción de edad, su tiempo como Residente Permanente no tiene que ser continuo. Se califica para una excepción si su tiempo total de residir como Residente Permanente en los Estados Unidos cae al menos entre 15 a 20 años.

Incapacidad: Si usted tiene una incapacidad física o de desarrollo o una debilitación mental, usted se puede calificar para una excepción a los requisitos de la prueba de inglés y de los estudios cívicos. Para solicitar una excepción, la incapacidad suya debe haber durado o se espera que dure a lo menos 12 meses, y no debe haber sido causado por el uso de drogas ilegales.

Para pedir una excepción, usted debe iniciar el "Certificado Médico Para las Excepciones de la Incapacidad" (Formulario N-648) junto con su solicitud para la naturalización. Si piensa que se califique, comuníquese con un médico licenciado o con un psicólogo quien necesitará llenar y firmar el formulario N-648.

> **¡Importante!** Una excepción médica del requisito del examen inglés y estudios cívicos *no le exime* del Juramento. A pesar de cualquier incapacidad, si usted no puede tomar y comprender el Juramento de Fidelidad, no es usted elegible para la ciudadanía.

English and civics requirements

According to the law, naturalization applicants must demonstrate English proficiency and civics knowledge:

- **English:** Understanding of the English language, including an ability to read, write and speak. The applicant must be able to communicate using simple words and phrases considered ordinary usage in the English language.

and

- **Civics:** A knowledge and understanding of the fundamentals of the history of the United States and the principles and form of the U.S government.

There are *exceptions* to these requirements for certain applicants due to age or disability, which are as follows:

Age: For English and civics testing, these are some exceptions based on the applicant's age at the time of filing.

- No English test if you are *over 50* years old and have lived in the United States as a Permanent Resident for periods totaling at least 20 years. You do have to take the civics test but may take it in the language of your choice.

- No English test if you are *over 55* years old and have lived in the United States as a Permanent Resident for periods totaling at least 15 years. You do have to take the civics test but can take it in the language of your choice.

- No English test if you are *over 65* years old and have lived in the United States as a Permanent Resident for periods totaling at least 20 years. You do have to take the civics test but can take it in the language of your choice. A simpler version of the civics test can also be taken.

You must meet these requirements at the time you file your application. To qualify for an age exemption, your time as a Permanent Resident does not have to be continuous. You are eligible for an exemption as long as your total time residing as a U.S. Permanent Resident is at least 15 to 20 years.

Disability: If you have a physical or developmental disability or mental impairment, you may be eligible for an exception to the English and civics testing requirements. To apply for a disability exception, your disability must have lasted or is expected to last for at least 12 months and must not have been caused by illegal drug use.

Enlace con la Constitución

Todos los solicitantes para la naturalización necesitan estar dispuestos a apoyar y defender los Estados Unidos y la Constitución. Cuando usted toma el Juramento de Fidelidad, está declarando en aquel tiempo su "enlace." Véase más información en el Capítulo Cuatro.

To request an exception, you must file a "Medical Certificate for Disability Exceptions" (Form N-648) along with your naturalization application. If you believe you qualify, contact a licensed medical doctor or psychologist who will need to complete and sign your N-648 form.

> **Important!** A medical exception from the English and civics requirement *does not exempt* you from the oath. Regardless of any disability, if you cannot take and understand the meaning of the Oath of Allegiance, then you are not eligible for citizenship.

Attachment to the Constitution

All applicants for naturalization must be willing to support and defend the United States and the Constitution. When you take the Oath of Allegiance, you are at that time declaring your "attachment." See Chapter Four for more information.

Capítulo Dos
La Solicitud

A la solicitud básica se le conoce como la **"Solicitud Para La Naturalización,"** **Formulario N-400,** y es lo que se usa la mayoría de los ciudadanos anticipados. A eso, se enfoca este capítulo.

Hay una solicitud diferente que se usan las personas que creen que hayan *derivido* la ciudadanía por medio de otra persona, como uno de los padres. Si se encuentra en esta situación, utilice la "Solicitud para el Certificado de la Ciudadanía," Formulario N-600, para obtener prueba de su ciudadanía. La información y las instrucciones para usar esta solicitud se encuentran al final de este capítulo.

Hay una tercera solicitud que se usan los ciudadanos de los Estados Unidos que han adoptado a un niño extranjero, "Solicitud para Certificado de Ciudadanía a Favor de un Niño Adoptado," Formulario N-643. Esta solicitud es fuera del alcance de este libro, pero el formulario y la información acerca de ella se puede conseguir por medio del INS.

Solicitud para la Naturalización (N-400)

La "Solicitud para la Naturalización," Formulario N-400, es la que usa usted cuando solicita su *propia* naturalización. Junto con el formulario N-400, usted debe entregar dos fotografías de usted, una fotocopia de cada lado de su Tarjeta de Residente Permanente, y un cheque o giro postal para el trámite de la solicitud. Más información sobre ellos aparece más adelante en este capítulo.

Cuando hacer la solicitud de naturalización

Quizás algunos inmigrantes quieran volverse ciudadanos lo más pronto posible. Otros pueden vivir en los Estados Unidos por años, aun por la mayor parte de sus vidas, antes de decidir volverse en ciudadanos. Aunque nunca es demasiado tarde para comenzar a hacer el proceso de solicitud, es posible comenzar demasiado temprano. Cuando usted decida, asegúrese de que se cumple con los requisitos de la naturalización especificados en el Capítulo Uno.

Para mayor eficiencia, usted puede conseguir una solicitud y comenzar a llenarla unos cuantos meses antes de cumplir con su requisito de residencia continua. Es una solicitud larga y toma mucho tiempo para llenarla. El INS se permite que una persona entregue su solicitud hasta 3 meses *antes* de la fecha actual en que

Chapter Two
The Application

The basic application is called the **"Application for Naturalization," Form N-400**, and that is what most prospective citizens use. Thus, it is the focus of this chapter.

There is a different application that is used by people who believe they have *derived* citizenship from somebody else, like a parent. If you are in this situation, use the "Application for Certificate of Citizenship," Form N-600, to get proof of your citizenship. Information and instructions for using this application are at the end of this chapter.

There is a third application that is used by U.S. citizens who have adopted a foreign child, "Application for Certificate of Citizenship in Behalf of an Adopted Child," Form N-643. This application is beyond the scope of this book, but the form and information about it are available from the INS. See Chapter One for how to obtain an application from the INS.

Application for Naturalization (N-400)

The "Application for Naturalization," Form N-400, is the one you submit to the INS to apply for your *own* naturalization. Along with the Form N-400, you must submit two photographs of yourself, a photocopy of both sides of your Permanent Resident Card, and a check or money order for filing your application. More information on these items appear later in this chapter.

When to apply for naturalization

Some immigrants may wish to become citizens at the earliest possible time. Others may live in the United States for years, maybe even most of their lives, before deciding to become citizens. While it is never too late to begin the application process, it is possible to begin too early. Whenever you decide, be certain that you meet the naturalization requirements specified in Chapter One.

For extra efficiency, you can get an application and begin filling it out a few months prior to meeting your continuous residence requirement. It is a lengthy application and takes considerable time to fill out. The INS does allow a person to submit his or her application up to 3 months *before* the date of actually meeting the "continuous residence" requirement. Timing it this way is a good plan for those desiring to apply for citizenship at the earliest possible time.

él o ella cumpla con el requisito de "residencia continua." Calculándolo de esta manera es buena idea para las personas que quieran hacer solicitud de ciudadanía lo más pronto posible.

Considere que una vez que usted haya sometido la solicitud, toma una cantidad de tiempo sustancial para ser procesada. El INS se ha anunciado que está tratando de reducir el período de esperar hasta 6 meses. En este momento, el tiempo para procesar la solicitud dura entre 6 a 12 meses o más. Se varia según la región geográfica. Así que tan pronto como reciba su solicitud el INS, más pronto será procesada.

Cómo llenar la solicitud

Las primeras seis páginas que vienen con el Formulario N-400, "Solicitud para la Naturalización" son instrucciones sobre la manera de llenarlo. Siga las instrucciones cuidadosamente y exactamente.

Escriba con letra de molde, claro y con letra MAYUSCULA, usando solamente tinta negra o azul (ningún otro color). Por supuesto, el uso de una máquina de escribir o computadora para llenar su solicitud es ideal. Para los que escojan usar una computadora, hay un formulario N-400, que se puede "llenar" disponible del sitio del internet del INS.

Instrucciones generales: Todos los artículos en el formulario deben ser respondidos lo mejor posible. Si una pregunta no se aplica a usted, no la deje en blanco. Preferiblemente, escriba "N/A" para *"not applicable."* Si necesita más espacio para contestar una pregunta, entonces agregue una hoja separada con esta información adicional. Para facilitarlo para usted, han proporcionado una hoja de *Información Adicional* en blanco para su uso detrás de la Solicitud N-400 en el Apéndice Cinco. La página proporciona a los espacios para escribir su nombre, su número de Residente Permanente (A#), y para indicar el número de la pregunta en que pertenece la información adicional.

Un ejemplo del Formulario N-400 completamente llenado empieza en la página siguiente (Muestra 1). Cuando escribe su número de Residente Permanente (PR), asegúrese de que tiene precisamente *nueve* números en total. Si su número de PR tiene menos de nueve dígitos, *agregue zeros* al principio. Por ejemplo:

$$A \underline{1}\,\underline{2}\,\underline{3}\,\underline{4}\,\underline{5}\,\underline{6}\,\underline{7} \text{ se debe escribir como } A \underline{0}\,\underline{0}\,\underline{1}\,\underline{2}\,\underline{3}\,\underline{4}\,\underline{5}\,\underline{6}\,\underline{7}$$

¡**Importante!** Si alguien le ayuda a usted a completar el Formulario N-400, asegúrese de que usted entiende totalmente cada pregunta y las ha contestado completamente y con exactitud porque estas preguntas y respuestas en su solicitud serán una parte importante de su examen de naturalización.

Monmouth Public Library

Title: Pasa el examen de
ciudadanía americana
Item ID: 33610033283570
Date due: 10/10/2017,23:
59

Title: How to become a
United States citizen : a
step-by
Item ID: 33610028623376
Date due: 10/10/2017,23:
59

.
.
.
Thank you

Bear in mind that once your application has been submitted, it takes a substantial amount of time to be processed. The INS has announced they are working at reducing this time period to six months. Currently, processing times are 6 to 12 months or longer. It varies depending on geographic regions. Therefore, the sooner the INS receives your application, the sooner it will be processed.

How to complete the application

The first six pages that come with your Form N-400, "Application for Naturalization," are instructions on how to fill it out. Follow the instructions carefully and exactly. Print neatly in all CAPITAL letters using only *black* or *blue* ink (no other color). Of course, use of a typewriter or a computer to complete your application would be ideal. For those opting to use a computer, a "fillable" N-400 is available from the INS website.

General Instructions: All items on the application should be answered to the best of your ability. If a question does not apply to you, do not leave it blank. Instead, write "N/A" for "not applicable." Should you need additional space to complete a question, then attach a separate sheet containing this additional information. To make this easy for you to do, a blank *Additional Information* sheet has been provided for your use following the N-400 Application in Appendix Five. The page provides spaces for you to fill in your name, Permanent Resident number (A#), and indicate the question number your additional information pertains to.

An example of the Form N-400 completely filled out begins on the next page (Sample 1). Be sure that when you write in your Permanent Resident (PR) number that it has exactly *nine* numbers total. If your PR number has *less* than nine digits, *add zeros* at the beginning. For example:

$$A \underline{1}\,\underline{2}\,\underline{3}\,\underline{4}\,\underline{5}\,\underline{6}\,\underline{7} \text{ should be written as } A \underline{0}\,\underline{0}\,\underline{1}\,\underline{2}\,\underline{3}\,\underline{4}\,\underline{5}\,\underline{6}\,\underline{7}$$

> **Important!** If someone helps you fill out the Form N-400, make sure that you fully understand every question and have answered each one accurately and completely because these questions and answers will be an important part of your naturalization examination.

Sample 1: Form N-400
Application for Naturalization (Page 1)

U.S. Department of Justice
Immigration and Naturalization Service

OMB No. 1115-0009

Application for Naturalization

Print clearly or type your answers using CAPITAL letters. Failure to print clearly may delay your application. Use black or blue ink.

Part 1. Your Name *(The Person Applying for Naturalization)*

A. Your current legal name.

Family Name *(Last Name)*

GONZALES

Given Name *(First Name)*

PEDRO

Full Middle Name *(If applicable)*

N/A

B. Your name exactly as it appears on your Permanent Resident Card.

Family Name *(Last Name)*

GONZALES

Given Name *(First Name)*

PEDRO

Full Middle Name *(If applicable)*

N/A

C. If you have ever used other names, provide them below.

Family Name *(Last Name)*	Given Name *(First Name)*	Middle Name
N/A		

D. Name change *(optional)*

Please read the Instructions before you decide whether to change your name.

1. Would you like to legally change your name? ☑ Yes ☐ No

2. If "Yes," print the new name you would like to use. Do not use initials or abbreviations when writing your new name.

Family Name *(Last Name)*

GONZALES

Given Name *(First Name)*

PETE

Full Middle Name

N/A

Write your INS "A"- number here:

A 028256001

FOR INS USE ONLY

Bar Code	Date Stamp

Remarks

Action

Part 2. Information About Your Eligibility *(Check Only One)*

I am at least 18 years old **AND**

A. ☑ I have been a Lawful Permanent Resident of the United States for at least 5 years.

B. ☐ I have been a Lawful Permanent Resident of the United States for at least 3 years, AND I have been married to and living with the same U.S. citizen for the last 3 years, AND my spouse has been a U.S. citizen for the last 3 years.

C. ☐ I am applying on the basis of qualifying military service.

D. ☐ Other *(Please explain)* _____

Form N-400 (Rev. 05/31/01)N

Form N-400
Application for Naturalization (Page 2)

Write your INS "A"- number here:
A 028256001

A. Social Security Number
555-12-3456

B. Date of Birth (Month/Day/Year)
08/28/1973

C. Date You Became a Permanent Resident (Month/Day/Year)
01/21/1996

D. Country of Birth
MEXICO

E. Country of Nationality
MEXICO

F. Are either of your parents U.S. citizens? (if yes, see Instructions) ☐ Yes ☑ No

G. What is your current marital status? ☐ Single, Never Married ☑ Married ☐ Divorced ☐ Widowed

☐ Marriage Annulled or Other (Explain) _____

H. Are you requesting a waiver of the English and/or U.S. History and Government requirements based on a disability or impairment and attaching a Form N-648 with your application? ☐ Yes ☑ No

I. Are you requesting an accommodation to the naturalization process because of a disability or impairment? (See Instructions for some examples of accommodations.) ☐ Yes ☑ No

If you answered "Yes", check the box below that applies:

☐ I am deaf or hearing impaired and need a sign language interpreter who uses the following language: _____

☐ I use a wheelchair.

☐ I am blind or sight impaired.

☐ I will need another type of accommodation. Please explain: _____

_____

Part 4. Addresses and Telephone Numbers

A. Home Address - Street Number and Name (Do NOT write a P.O. Box in this space)
621 E. EMMETT STREET

Apartment Number
N/A

City: SANTA ANA
County: ORANGE
State: CA
ZIP Code: 92799
Country: U.S.A.

B. Care of
N/A

Mailing Address - Street Number and Name (If different from home address)
SAME

Apartment Number

City
State
ZIP Code
Country

C. Daytime Phone Number (If any)
( ) N/A

Evening Phone Number (If any)
(714) 123-4567

E-mail Address (If any)
N/A

Form N-400 (Rev. 05/31/01)N Page 2

Form N-400
Application for Naturalization (Page 3)

Part 5. Information for Criminal Records Search

Write your INS "A"- number here:
A 028256001

Note: The categories below are those required by the FBI. See Instructions for more information.

A. Gender

[✓] Male   [ ] Female

B. Height

5 Feet 11 Inches

C. Weight

178 Pounds

D. Race

[✓] White   [ ] Asian or Pacific Islander   [ ] Black   [ ] American Indian or Alaskan Native   [ ] Unknown

E. Hair color

[✓] Black   [ ] Brown   [ ] Blonde   [ ] Gray   [ ] White   [ ] Red   [ ] Sandy   [ ] Bald (No Hair)

F. Eye color

[ ] Brown   [ ] Blue   [✓] Green   [ ] Hazel   [ ] Gray   [ ] Black   [ ] Pink   [ ] Maroon   [ ] Other

Part 6. Information About Your Residence and Employment

A. Where have you lived during the last 5 years? Begin with where you live now and then list every place you lived for the last 5 years. If you need more space, use a separate sheet of paper.

Street Number and Name, Apartment Number, City, State, Zip Code and Country	Dates (Month/Year) From	To
Current Home Address - Same as Part 4.A	02/1996	Present
621 E. EMMETT STREET	__/____	__/____
SANTA ANA CALIF. 92799	__/____	__/____
U.S.A.	__/____	__/____
	__/____	__/____

B. Where have you worked (or, if you were a student, what schools did you attend) during the last 5 years? Include military service. Begin with your current or latest employer and then list every place you have worked or studied for the last 5 years. If you need more space, use a separate sheet of paper.

Employer or School Name	Employer or School Address (Street, City and State)	Dates (Month/Year) From	To	Your Occupation
PRECISION AUTOMOTIVE	175 MAIN STREET SANTA ANA CALIF.	03/1996	PRESENT	MECHANIC
		__/____	__/____	
		__/____	__/____	
		__/____	__/____	
		__/____	__/____	

Form N-400 (Rev. 05/31/01)N Page 3

Form N-400
Application for Naturalization (Page 4)

Part 7. Time Outside the United States
(Including Trips to Canada, Mexico, and the Caribbean Islands)

Write your INS "A"- number here:
A 0 2 8 2 5 6 0 0 1

A. How many total days did you spend outside of the United States during the past 5 years? **21** days

B. How many trips of 24 hours or more have you taken outside of the United States during the past 5 years? **3** trips

C. List below all the trips of 24 hours or more that you have taken outside of the United States since becoming a Lawful Permanent Resident. Begin with your most recent trip. If you need more space, use a separate sheet of paper.

Date You Left the United States (Month/Day/Year)	Date You Returned to the United States (Month/Day/Year)	Did Trip Last 6 Months or More?	Countries to Which You Traveled	Total Days Out of the United States
12/23/2000	01/03/2001	☐Yes ☑No	MEXICO	11
12/20/1999	12/26/1999	☐Yes ☑No	MEXICO	6
08/16/1998	08/20/1998	☐Yes ☑No	MEXICO	4
/ /	/ /	☐Yes ☐No		
/ /	/ /	☐Yes ☐No		
/ /	/ /	☐Yes ☐No		
/ /	/ /	☐Yes ☐No		
/ /	/ /	☐Yes ☐No		
/ /	/ /	☐Yes ☐No		
/ /	/ /	☐Yes ☐No		

Part 8. Information About Your Marital History

A. How many times have you been married (including annulled marriages)? **1** If you have NEVER been married, go to Part 9.

B. If you are now married, give the following information about your spouse:

1. Spouse's Family Name *(Last Name)*: **HERNANDEZ** Given Name *(First Name)*: **MARIA** Full Middle Name *(If applicable)*: **ESCANDON**

2. Date of Birth *(Month/Day/Year)*: **11/25/1974** 3. Date of Marriage *(Month/Day/Year)*: **06/01/1998** 4. Spouse's Social Security Number: **555-11-2233**

5. Home Address - Street Number and Name: **621 E. EMMETT STREET** Apartment Number: **N/A**

City: **SANTA ANA** State: **CALIFORNIA** ZIP Code: **92799**

Form N-400 (Rev. 05/31/01)N Page 4

Form N-400
Application for Naturalization (Page 5)

Part 8. Information About Your Marital History *(Continued)*

Write your INS "A"- number here:
A 028 256 001

C. Is your spouse a U.S. citizen?   ☐ Yes   ☑ No

D. If your spouse is a U.S. citizen, give the following information: N/A

    1. When did your spouse become a U.S. citizen?   ☐ At Birth   ☐ Other

    If "Other," give the following information:

    2. Date your spouse became a U.S. citizen

    3. Place your spouse became a U.S. citizen *(Please see Instructions)*

    City and State

E. If your spouse is NOT a U.S. citizen, give the following information :

    1. Spouse's Country of Citizenship

    MEXICO

    2. Spouse's INS "A"- Number *(If applicable)*

    A 002825611

    3. Spouse's Immigration Status

    ☑ Lawful Permanent Resident   ☐ Other

F. If you were married before, provide the following information about your prior spouse. If you have more than one previous marriage, use a separate sheet of paper to provide the information requested in questions 1-5 below. N/A

    1. Prior Spouse's Family Name *(Last Name)*   Given Name *(First Name)*   Full Middle Name *(If applicable)*

    2. Prior Spouse's Immigration Status

    ☐ U.S. Citizen

    ☐ Lawful Permanent Resident

    ☐ Other

    3. Date of Marriage *(Month/Day/Year)*

    4. Date Marriage Ended *(Month/Day/Year)*

    5. How Marriage Ended

    ☐ Divorce   ☐ Spouse Died   ☐ Other

G. How many times has your current spouse been married (including annulled marriages)?   0

    If your spouse has EVER been married before, give the following information about your spouse's prior marriage.
    If your spouse has more than one previous marriage, use a separate sheet of paper to provide the information requested in questions 1 - 5 below.

    1. Prior Spouse's Family Name *(Last Name)*   Given Name *(First Name)*   Full Middle Name *(If applicable)*

    2. Prior Spouse's Immigration Status

    ☐ U.S. Citizen

    ☐ Lawful Permanent Resident

    ☐ Other

    3. Date of Marriage *(Month/Day/Year)*

    4. Date Marriage Ended *(Month/Day/Year)*

    5. How Marriage Ended

    ☐ Divorce   ☐ Spouse Died   ☐ Other

Form N-400 (Rev. 05/31/01)N Page 5

Form N-400
Application for Naturalization (Page 6)

Part 9. Information About Your Children	Write your INS "A"- number here:
	A 028256001

A. How many sons and daughters have you had? For more information on which sons and daughters you should include and how to complete this section, see the Instructions. `2`

B. Provide the following information about all of your sons and daughters. If you need more space, use a separate sheet of paper.

Full Name of Son or Daughter	Date of Birth (Month/Day/Year)	INS "A"- number (if child has one)	Country of Birth	Current Address (Street, City, State & Country)
CELINA MARIA	01/14/2001	A N/A	U.S.A.	(WITH ME)
ROBERTO PEDRO GONZALES	01/14/2001	A N/A	U.S.A.	(WITH ME)
	__/__/____	A_____		
	__/__/____	A_____		
	__/__/____	A_____		
	__/__/____	A_____		
	__/__/____	A_____		
	__/__/____	A_____		

Part 10. Additional Questions

Please answer questions 1 through 14. If you answer "Yes" to any of these questions, include a written explanation with this form. Your written explanation should (1) explain why your answer was "Yes," and (2) provide any additional information that helps to explain your answer.

A. General Questions

1. Have you **EVER** claimed to be a U.S. citizen *(in writing or any other way)*? ☐ Yes ☑ No
2. Have you **EVER** registered to vote in any Federal, state, or local election in the United States? ☐ Yes ☑ No
3. Have you **EVER** voted in any Federal, state, or local election in the United States? ☐ Yes ☑ No
4. Since becoming a Lawful Permanent Resident, have you **EVER** failed to file a required Federal, state, or local tax return? ☐ Yes ☑ No
5. Do you owe any Federal, state, or local taxes that are overdue? ☐ Yes ☑ No
6. Do you have any title of nobility in any foreign country? ☐ Yes ☑ No
7. Have you ever been declared legally incompetent or been confined to a mental institution within the last 5 years? ☐ Yes ☑ No

Form N-400 (Rev. 05/31/01)N Page 6

Form N-400
Application for Naturalization (Page 7)

Part 10. Additional Questions *(Continued)*

Write your INS "A"- number here:
A 028256001

B. Affiliations

8. a. Have you **EVER** been a member of or associated with any organization, association, fund, foundation, party, club, society, or similar group in the United States or in any other place? ☑ Yes ☐ No

b. If you answered "Yes," list the name of each group below. If you need more space, attach the names of the other group(s) on a separate sheet of paper.

Name of Group	Name of Group
1. ST. CECILIA'S CATHOLIC CHURCH	6.
2. ORANGE COUNTY CHAPTER AMERICAN RED CROSS	7.
3. AUTO MECHANICS ASSOC.	8.
4.	9.
5.	10.

9. Have you **EVER** been a member of or in any way associated *(either directly or indirectly)* with:

   a. The Communist Party? ☐ Yes ☑ No

   b. Any other totalitarian party? ☐ Yes ☑ No

   c. A terrorist organization? ☐ Yes ☑ No

10. Have you **EVER** advocated *(either directly or indirectly)* the overthrow of any government by force or violence? ☐ Yes ☑ No

11. Have you **EVER** persecuted *(either directly or indirectly)* any person because of race, religion, national origin, membership in a particular social group, or political opinion? ☐ Yes ☑ No

12. Between March 23, 1933, and May 8, 1945, did you work for or associate in any way *(either directly or indirectly)* with:

   a. The Nazi government of Germany? ☐ Yes ☑ No

   b. Any government in any area (1) occupied by, (2) allied with, or (3) established with the help of the Nazi government of Germany? ☐ Yes ☑ No

   c. Any German, Nazi, or S.S. military unit, paramilitary unit, self-defense unit, vigilante unit, citizen unit, police unit, government agency or office, extermination camp, concentration camp, prisoner of war camp, prison, labor camp, or transit camp? ☐ Yes ☑ No

C. Continuous Residence

Since becoming a Lawful Permanent Resident of the United States:

13. Have you **EVER** called yourself a "nonresident" on a Federal, state, or local tax return? ☐ Yes ☑ No

14. Have you **EVER** failed to file a Federal, state, or local tax return because you considered yourself to be a "nonresident"? ☐ Yes ☑ No

Form N-400 (Rev. 05/31/01)N Page 7

Form N-400
Application for Naturalization (Page 8)

Part 10. Additional Questions *(Continued)*

D. Good Moral Character

For the purposes of this application, you must answer "Yes" to the following questions, if applicable, even if your records were sealed or otherwise cleared or if anyone, including a judge, law enforcement officer, or attorney, told you that you no longer have a record.

15. Have you **EVER** committed a crime or offense for which you were NOT arrested? ☐ Yes ☑ No

16. Have you **EVER** been arrested, cited, or detained by any law enforcement officer (including INS and military officers) for any reason? ☑ Yes ☐ No

17. Have you **EVER** been charged with committing any crime or offense? ☐ Yes ☑ No

18. Have you **EVER** been convicted of a crime or offense? ☐ Yes ☑ No

19. Have you **EVER** been placed in an alternative sentencing or a rehabilitative program (for example: diversion, deferred prosecution, withheld adjudication, deferred adjudication)? ☐ Yes ☑ No

20. Have you **EVER** received a suspended sentence, been placed on probation, or been paroled? ☐ Yes ☑ No

21. Have you **EVER** been in jail or prison? ☐ Yes ☑ No

If you answered "Yes" to any of questions 15 through 21, complete the following table. If you need more space, use a separate sheet of paper to give the same information.

Why were you arrested, cited, detained, or charged?	Date arrested, cited, detained, or charged *(Month/Day/Year)*	Where were you arrested, cited, detained or charged? *(City, State, Country)*	Outcome or disposition of the arrest, citation, detention or charge *(No charges filed, charges dismissed, jail, probation, etc.)*
DISTURBING THE PEACE	05/30/1998	CITED	CHARGES DISMISSED

Answer questions 22 through 33. If you answer "Yes" to any of these questions, attach (1) your written explanation why your answer was "Yes," and (2) any additional information or documentation that helps explain your answer.

22. Have you **EVER**:

a. been a habitual drunkard? ☐ Yes ☑ No

b. been a prostitute, or procured anyone for prostitution? ☐ Yes ☑ No

c. sold or smuggled controlled substances, illegal drugs or narcotics? ☐ Yes ☑ No

d. been married to more than one person at the same time? ☐ Yes ☑ No

e. helped anyone enter or try to enter the United States illegally? ☐ Yes ☑ No

f. gambled illegally or received income from illegal gambling? ☐ Yes ☑ No

g. failed to support your dependents or to pay alimony? ☐ Yes ☑ No

23. Have you **EVER** given false or misleading information to any U.S. government official while applying for any immigration benefit or to prevent deportation, exclusion, or removal? ☐ Yes ☑ No

24. Have you **EVER** lied to any U.S. government official to gain entry or admission into the United States? ☐ Yes ☑ No

Form N-400 (Rev. 05/31/01)N Page 8

Form N-400
Application for Naturalization (Page 9)

Part 10. Additional Questions *(Continued)*	Write your INS "A"- number here:
	A 0 2 8 2 5 6 0 0 1

E. Removal, Exclusion, and Deportation Proceedings

25. Are removal, exclusion, rescission or deportation proceedings pending against you? ☐Yes ☑No

26. Have you **EVER** been removed, excluded, or deported from the United States? ☐Yes ☑No

27. Have you **EVER** been ordered to be removed, excluded, or deported from the United States? ☐Yes ☑No

28. Have you **EVER** applied for any kind of relief from removal, exclusion, or deportation? ☐Yes ☑No

F. Military Service

29. Have you **EVER** served in the U.S. Armed Forces? ☐Yes ☑No

30. Have you **EVER** left the United States to avoid being drafted into the U.S. Armed Forces? ☐Yes ☑No

31. Have you **EVER** applied for any kind of exemption from military service in the U.S. Armed Forces? ☐Yes ☑No

32. Have you **EVER** deserted from the U.S. Armed Forces? ☐Yes ☑No

G. Selective Service Registration

33. Are you a male who lived in the United States at any time between your 18th and 26th birthdays in any status except as a lawful nonimmigrant? ☐Yes ☑No

If you answered "NO", go on to question 34.

If you answered "YES", provide the information below.

If you answered "YES", but you did NOT register with the Selective Service System and are still under 26 years of age, you must register before you apply for naturalization, so that you can complete the information below:

Date Registered (Month/Day/Year) [   ]   Selective Service Number [__ __ / __ __ __ / __ __ __ __]

If you answered "YES", but you did NOT register with the Selective Service and you are now 26 years old or older, attach a statement explaining why you did not register.

H. Oath Requirements *(See Part 14 for the text of the oath)*

Answer questions 34 through 39. If you answer "No" to any of these questions, attach (1) your written explanation why the answer was "No" and (2) any additional information or documentation that helps to explain your answer.

34. Do you support the Constitution and form of government of the United States? ☑Yes ☐No

35. Do you understand the full Oath of Allegiance to the United States? ☑Yes ☐No

36. Are you willing to take the full Oath of Allegiance to the United States? ☑Yes ☐No

37. If the law requires it, are you willing to bear arms on behalf of the United States? ☑Yes ☐No

38. If the law requires it, are you willing to perform noncombatant services in the U.S. Armed Forces? ☑Yes ☐No

39. If the law requires it, are you willing to perform work of national importance under civilian direction? ☑Yes ☐No

Form N-400 (Rev. 05/31/01)N Page 9

Form N-400
Application for Naturalization (Page 10)

Part 11. Your Signature

Write your INS "A"- number here:
A _028256001_

I certify, under penalty of perjury under the laws of the United States of America, that this application, and the evidence submitted with it, are all true and correct. I authorize the release of any information which INS needs to determine my eligibility for naturalization.

Your Signature

Pedro Gonzales

Date *(Month/Day/Year)*

_06|23|2001_

Part 12. Signature of Person Who Prepared This Application for You (if applicable)

I declare under penalty of perjury that I prepared this application at the request of the above person. The answers provided are based on information of which I have personal knowledge and/or were provided to me by the above named person in response to the *exact questions* contained on this form.

Preparer's Printed Name

Preparer's Signature

Date *(Month/Day/Year)*

Preparer's Firm or Organization Name *(If applicable)*

Preparer's Daytime Phone Number
( )

Preparer's Address - Street Number and Name

City

State

ZIP Code

Do Not Complete Parts 13 and 14 Until an INS Officer Instructs You To Do So

Part 13. Signature at Interview

I swear (affirm) and certify under penalty of perjury under the laws of the United States of America th~~at~~ application for naturalization subscribed by me, including corrections numbered 1 throu~~gh~~ numbered pages 1 through _____, are true and correct to the best of my knowle~~dge~~

Subscribed to and sworn to (affirmed) before me

Day/Year)

Complete Signature of Applicant

DO NOT COMPLETE UNTIL INSTRUCTED TO DO SO

Part 14. Oath of Alle~~giance~~

If your application is appr~~oved~~ ~~for~~ a public oath ceremony at which time you will be required to take the following oath of allegiance immedia~~tely~~ ~~becomin~~g a naturalized citizen. By signing below, you acknowledge your willingness and ability to take this oath:

I hereby declare, on oath, that I absolutely and entirely renounce and abjure all allegiance and fidelity to any foreign prince, potentate, state, or sovereignty, of whom or which which I have heretofore been a subject or citizen;

that I will support and defend the Constitution and laws of the United States of America against all enemies, foreign and domestic;
that I will bear true faith and allegiance to the same;
that I will bear arms on behalf of the United States when required by the law;
that I will perform noncombatant service in the Armed Forces of the United States when required by the law;
that I will perform work of national importance under civilian direction when required by the law; and
that I take this obligation freely, without any mental reservation or purpose of evasion; so help me God.

Printed Name of Applicant

Complete Signature of Applicant

Form N-400 (Rev. 05/31/01)N Page 10

Fotografías

Usted necesitará entregar 2 fotografías de color de usted mismo sacadas *no antes de 30 días* antes de someter su solicitud. Usted encontrará que casi siempre los salones fotográficos son familiares con las especificaciones de la foto del INS. Sin embargo, para estar seguro, lleve con usted las especificaciones (véase la Muestra 2) cuando vaya a retratarse. El costo generalmente está bajo $15.00. Se recomienda que primero llame al fotógrafo que haya usted seleccionado para preguntar si una cita es necesaria. La mayoría de los fotógrafos son capaces de tomar las fotos instantáneas y tenerlas listas en unos minutos. Necesitará escribir su nombre y número de Residente Permanente con lápiz en la parte posterior de cada foto. Tenga cuidado de no escribir demasiado fuerte al escribir en la parte posterior para evitar el dañar de ellas.

Huellas dactilares

Las huellas dactilares se registran y después se envían a la Oficina Federal de Investigaciones (FBI), para el análisis de involucramiento posterior posible en conducta delictiva. A las personas que superan los 75 años de edad en el tiempo de la solicitud, se les exime del requisito de la huella dactilar. Dependiendo de donde usted reside, se determina *cuando* y *cómo* usted somete las huellas dactilares:

Solicitantes que residen en los *Estados Unidos:* Se le exige primero que usted entregue su solicitud terminada N-400 con el INS. Luego, usted recibirá una carta para una cita del INS que le dice *cuando* y *adonde* ir a tomar sus huellas dactilares. Generalmente, dirigirán a los solicitantes a un Centro Local de Apoyo del Solicitante del INS.

En el día determinado para la cita de tomar las huellas dactilares, tome con usted su carta de cita del INS, su Tarjeta de Residente Permanente y otra forma de identificación tal como una licencia de manejar o tarjeta estatal de identificación con su fotografía en ella. ¡Llegue a la *hora debida* para su cita! Si usted no puede asistir la cita señalada, llame la oficina del INS de antemano para cambiar la hora. Con la excepción de emergencias calamitosas, *no* cambie la hora. Esto sólo retrasará más lejos el proceso ya muy largo de la naturalización.

Solicitantes que residen en el *extranjero:* Un formulario llenado (FD-258) de la tarjeta de la huella dactilar debe ser *incluido* cuando usted somete la solicitud N-400 al INS. Los solicitantes de ultramar deben tener sus tarjetas de la huella dactilar preparadas en una oficina Consular de los EE.UU. o una base militar. Vea el *Apéndice Dos* para una muestra de tal tarjeta de la huella dactilar.

Photographs

You will need to submit 2 color photographs of yourself taken *no earlier than 30 days* before submitting your application. You will find that photography studios are usually very familiar with INS photo specifications. However, just to be on the safe side, take the specifications (see Sample 2) with you when you go to have your picture taken. The cost is usually under $15. It's recommended that you first call the photographer you have selected to ask if you need an appointment. Most photographers have the capability to take your picture and have the photos ready within minutes. You will need to write your name and Permanent Resident number in pencil on the back of each photo. Be careful not to press too hard when writing on the back of the photos to prevent damaging them.

Fingerprints

Fingerprints are recorded and then sent to the Federal Bureau of Investigation (FBI) for analysis of possible past involvement in criminal behavior. Persons 75 years of age or older at time of application are exempt from the fingerprinting requirement. Depending on where you reside determines *when* and *how* you submit the fingerprints:

Applicants residing in the *United States:* You are required to first file your completed N-400 application with the INS. Afterwards, you will receive an appointment letter from the INS telling you *when* and *where* to go to have your fingerprints taken. Usually applicants will be directed to a local INS Application Support Center.

On your scheduled fingerprinting appointment day, take with you your appointment letter from the INS, your Permanent Resident Card, and another form of identification such as a driver's license or state identification card with your photograph on it. Arrive *on time* to meet your appointment! If you cannot meet your designated appointment, contact the INS beforehand to reschedule. Except for dire emergencies, do *not* reschedule your appointment. This will just further delay the already lengthy naturalization process.

Applicants residing *overseas:* A completed fingerprint card form (FD-258) must be *included* when you submit your completed N-400 application to INS. Overseas applicants must have their fingerprint cards prepared at a U.S. Consular office or military base. See *Appendix Two* for a sample of such a fingerprint card.

La entrega de la solicitud completa

Se debe enviar a un Centro del Servicio del INS su solicitud completa N-400. Se puede iniciar la naturalización hasta 3 meses antes de que haya cumplido con el requisito de la "residencia continua." En este momento, el INS tiene 4 centros de servicio, cada uno de los cuales sirve una región geográfica determinada. Usted debe enviar su solicitud al centro de servicio que cubre la *área donde vive usted*. Una lista de estas direcciones está proporcionada en su Solicitud N-400 del INS y también en el Apendíce Cinco de este libro.

Se requiere que se incluyan los documentos siguientes cuando usted entrega su Solicitud N-400 para la Naturalización:

- Una copia de *los dos lados* de su Tarjeta de Residente Permanente.

- Dos fotografías de color como las de la Muestra 2.

- Un cheque o giro postal (no efectivo) pagadero al *Immigration and Naturalization Service*. O sea el Servicio de Inmigración y Naturalización. Para la tarifa actual, véase la "Tabla de Tarifas" que está en la parte interior de la cubierta de atrás.

- Las diez páginas enteras de la Solicitud de la Naturalización completa, Formulario N-400, y:

- *Copias* de cualesquier documentos justificativos *más* una declaración firmada que atestigua que son copias verdaderas, exactas e inalteradas de los documentos *originales*. (Un formulario de declaración y firma en blanco—*Información Importante del Documento*—se ha proporcionado para su uso detrás de la Solicitud N-400 en el Apéndice Cinco.)

En la pagina 44, usted verá ejemplos de los tipos de documentos justificativos que se requieren — por supuesto, sólo para esas circunstancias que se apliquen a su caso. No envíe ningún documento *original*. En lugar, envíe las copias de sus documentos. Sin embargo, espere que el INS le pida traer los originales a su cita de la entrevista.

Los solicitantes en el extranjero tienen las siguientes excepciones:

1. **Huellas dactilares:** Usted debe *incluir* una tarjeta completa de huellas dactilares, Formulario FD-258, *con* su solicitud N-400. Se debe hacer las huellas dactilares en una oficina Consular de los Estados Unidos o base militar.

2. **Costo de trámite solamente:** Su cheque o giro postal debe cubrir el costo del trámite *solamente*. No incluya el costo de la huella dactilar. (Vea por favor la "Tabla de Tarifas" que está en la parte interior de la cubierta de atrás de este libro).

Submitting the completed application

Your completed N-400 application *must be mailed to an INS Service Center*. You may file for naturalization up to 3 months before you have met your "continuous residence" requirement. Currently, the INS has 4 service centers, each of which handles a particular geographic region. You must mail your application to the service center *covering the area where you live*. A list of these addresses is provided in with your N-400 Application from the INS and also in Appendix Five of this book.

The filing of your Application for Naturalization requires the following items to be included with your N-400:

- A copy of *both* sides of your Permanent Resident Card;

- Two color photographs as in Sample 2;

- Your check or money order (not cash) made payable to the *Immigration and Naturalization Service*. For current amount, please refer to the "Fee Chart" on the inside back cover of this book.

- All 10 pages of the completed Application for Naturalization, Form N-400, and;

- *Copies* of any supporting documents *plus* a signed statement attesting that they are true, exact and unaltered copies of *original* documents. (A blank statement and signature forrm—*Important Document Information*—has been provided for your use after the tear-out N-400 Application in Appendix Five.)

On page 44, you will see examples of the kinds of supporting documents required—of course, only for those instances that apply to your case. Do not mail the *original* of any document. Instead, send *copies* of your documents. However, expect to be asked by the INS to bring the original(s) along to your interview appointment.

Overseas applicants have the following exceptions:

1. **Fingerprinting:** You must *include* a completed fingerprint card, Form FD-258, in *with* your N-400 application, and it must be done at a U.S. Consular office or military base.

2. **Filing fee only:** Your check or money order should be for the filing fee *only*. Do not include a fingerprinting fee. (Please refer to the "Fee Chart" on the inside back cover of this book.)

   a. **Guam applicants:** Make your check or money order payable to "Treasurer, Guam."

   b. **Virgin Islands applicants:** Make your check or money order payable to "Commissioner of Finance of the Virgin Islands."

a. **Solicitantes de Guam:** Haga su cheque o giro postal a nombre del "Treasurer, Guam" o sea "Tesorero de Guam."

b. **Solicitantes de las Islas Vírgenes:** Haga su cheque o giro postal a nombre del "Commissioner of Finance of the Virgin Islands." O sea, "Comisionado Financiero de las Islas Vírgenes."

Perdón del costo del trámite

Los solicitantes que no pueden cobrar el costo asociado a la naturalización, pueden ser elegibles para un perdón del costo. Por lo general, esto implica anexar una declaración jurada, o una declaración sin jurar, con la solicitud que pida el perdón del costo y declare los motivos especificados de por qué no le es posible pagar el costo. Necesitará incluir los documentos justificativos para *probar* su situación financiera. Comuníquese con el INS para más información específica sobre el perdón.

Enviar la solicitud por correo

¡Antes de enviar la solicitud, haga una copia de ella! Será una referencia valiosa en la preparación para su entrevista. Y será provechoso tener una copia en el caso de que se pierda su original. Además, traiga la copia consigo cuando vaya a la entrevista. Debido a la importancia de la solicitud, envíela por "Correo Certificado" con "Acuse de Recibo a Vuelta." Luego usted conseguirá una verificación que el INS, en hecho, sí recibió la solicitud. Es buena idea usar un sobre largo y plano, preferiblemente de 9 por 12 pulgadas, para enviar la solicitud original N-400 y el contenido. Luego, viene un período de espera, algunas veces de varios meses. Sin embargo, usted se puede emplear su tiempo de espera en algo positivo. Utilícelo para estudiar para la prueba de estudios cívicos o para practicar el inglés, si se necesita.

Solicitud para el Certificado de Ciudadanía (N-600)

La otra solicitud que se menciona al comienzo de este capítulo es el Formulario N-600, "Solicitud para el Certificado de Ciudadanía." Es para las personas que creen que ya son ciudadanos a través de otra persona, como uno de los padres o esposo(a), y quieren prueba escrita de su ciudadanía. El uso de este formulario es absolutamente voluntario y no afecta de ninguna manera la ciudadanía actual. Someta el formulario solamente si desea usted personalmente tener un certificado. El INS no lo requiere, pero lo proveen para ayudarle obtener prueba de la ciudadanía, si es lo que quiere hacer.

Sample 2: Photograph Specifications

U. S. IMMIGRATION & NATURALIZATION SERVICE

COLOR PHOTOGRAPH SPECIFICATIONS

IDEAL PHOTOGRAPH ◄

IMAGE MUST FIT INSIDE THIS BOX ►

THE PICTURE AT LEFT IS IDEAL SIZE, COLOR, BACKGROUND, AND POSE. THE IMAGE SHOULD BE 30MM (1 3/16IN) FROM THE HAIR TO JUST BELOW THE CHIN, AND 26MM (1 IN) FROM LEFT CHEEK TO RIGHT EAR. THE IMAGE MUST FIT IN THE BOX AT RIGHT.

THE PHOTOGRAPH
* THE OVERALL SIZE OF THE PICTURE, INCLUDING THE BACKGROUND, MUST BE AT LEAST 40MM (1 9/16 INCHES) IN HEIGHT BY 35MM (1 3/8IN) IN WIDTH.

* PHOTOS MUST BE FREE OF SHADOWS AND CONTAIN NO MARKS, SPLOTCHES, OR DISCOLORATIONS.

* PHOTOS SHOULD BE HIGH QUALITY, WITH GOOD BACK LIGHTING OR WRAP AROUND LIGHTING, AND MUST HAVE A WHITE OR OFF-WHITE BACKGROUND.

* PHOTOS MUST BE A GLOSSY OR MATTE FINISH AND UN-RETOUCHED.

* POLAROID FILM HYBRID #5 IS ACCEPTABLE; HOWEVER SX-70 TYPE FILM OR ANY OTHER INSTANT PROCESSING TYPE FILM IS UNACCEPTABLE. NON-PEEL APART FILMS ARE EASILY RECOGNIZED BECAUSE THE BACK OF THE FILM IS BLACK. ACCEPTABLE INSTANT COLOR FILM HAS A GRAY-TONED BACKING.

THE IMAGE OF THE PERSON
* THE DIMENSIONS OF THE IMAGE SHOULD BE 30MM (1 3/16 INCHES) FROM THE HAIR TO THE NECK JUST BELOW THE CHIN, AND 26MM (1 INCH) FROM THE RIGHT EAR TO THE LEFT CHEEK. IMAGE CANNOT EXCEED 32MM BY 28MM (1 1/4IN X 1 1/16IN).

* IF THE IMAGE AREA ON THE PHOTOGRAPH IS TOO LARGE OR TOO SMALL, THE PHOTO CANNOT BE USED.

* PHOTOGRAPHS MUST SHOW THE ENTIRE FACE OF THE PERSON IN A 3/4 VIEW SHOWING THE RIGHT EAR AND LEFT EYE.

* FACIAL FEATURES **MUST BE IDENTIFIABLE.**

* CONTRAST BETWEEN THE IMAGE AND BACKGROUND IS ESSENTIAL. PHOTOS FOR VERY LIGHT SKINNED PEOPLE SHOULD BE SLIGHTLY UNDER-EXPOSED. PHOTOS FOR VERY DARK SKINNED PEOPLE SHOULD BE SLIGHTLY OVER-EXPOSED.

SAMPLES OF UNACCEPTABLE PHOTOGRAPHS

INCORRECT POSE

IMAGE TOO LARGE

IMAGE TOO SMALL

IMAGE TOO DARK UNDER-EXPOSED

IMAGE TOO LIGHT

DARK BACKGROUND

OVER-EXPOSED

SHADOWS ON PIC

Immigration & Naturalization Service
Form M-378 (6-92)

Kinds of "supporting documents"

If your current name is different from the name on your Permanent Resident Card, send:

- The document which legally changed your name (marriage license, divorce decree, *or* court document), *or* a detailed explanation of why you use a different name.

If you were previously married, send:

- Proof of termination of *all* prior marriages (divorce decree *or* death certificate).

If you have a dependent spouse or children and have been ordered to provide financial support, send:

- Copies of the court or government order to provide financial support; *and*

- Evidence that you have complied with the court or government order (cancelled checks, money order receipts, a court or agency printout of child support payments, OR evidence of wage garnishments).

If you have failed to file an income tax return when it was required by law, send:

- Copies of all correspondence with the Internal Revenue Service (IRS) regarding your failure to file.

If you have any Federal, state, or local taxes that are overdue, send:

- A signed agreement from the IRS, state, or local tax office showing that you have filed a tax return and arranged to pay the taxes you owe, *and*

- Documentation from the IRS, state, or local tax office showing the current status of your repayment program.

If you have taken a trip outside the United States that lasted for 6 months or more since becoming a Permanent Resident, send:

- An original IRS Form 1722 listing tax information for the past 5 years (or for the past 3 years if you are applying on the basis or marriage to a U.S. citizen).

If you are applying for naturalization on the basis of marriage to a U.S. citizen, send:

- Proof that your spouse has been a U.S. citizen for at least the past 3 years (birth certificate, naturalization certificate, certificate of citizenship, copy of the inside front cover and signature page of your spouse's valid U.S. passport *or* Form FS240, "Report of Birth Abroad of a Citizen of the United States of America:);

- Your current marriage certificate;

- Proof of termination of *all* of your spouse's prior marriages (divorce decree *or* death certificate) *and*

- An original INS Form 1722 listing tax information for the past 3 years *or* copies of the income tax forms you filed for the past 3 years.

If you have ever been in the United States military, send:

- An original Form N-426, "Request for Certification of Military or Naval Service," *and*

- An original Form G-328B, "Biographic Information."

If you did not register with the Selective Service and you 1) are male, 2) are 26 years old or older, and 3) lived in the United States in a status other than as a lawful nonimmigrant between the ages of 18 and 26, send:

- A "Status Information Letter" from the Selective Service
  (call 1-847-688-6888 for more information).

If you have ever been arrested or detained by any law enforcement officer for any reason and no charges were filed, send:

- An official statement from the arresting agency or applicable court
  indicating that no charges were filed.

If you have ever been arrested or detained by any law enforcement officer for any reason and charges were filed, send:

- An original or certified copy of the complete court disposition for each incident
  (dismissal order, conviction record, OR acquittal order).

If you have ever been convicted or placed in an alternative sentencing program or rehabilitative program, send:

- The sentencing record for each incident, *and*

- Evidence that you completed your sentence (probation record, parole record, *or* evidence that you completed an alternative sentencing program or rehabilitative program).

If you have ever had any arrest or conviction vacated, set aside, sealed, expunged, or otherwise removed from your record, send:

- An original or certified copy of the court order vacating, setting aside, sealing, expunging, or otherwise removing the arrest or conviction.

If you are applying for a disability exception to the testing requirement, send:

- An original Form N-648, "Medical Certification for Disability Exceptions," completed by a licensed medical doctor or licensed clinical psychologist.

If an attorney or accredited representative is acting on your behalf, send:

- Form G-28, "Notice of Entry of Appearance as Attorney Representative."

Source: Immigration and Naturalization Service

Puesto que usted no está solicitando para *hacerse* ciudadano, no le requieren someter huellas dactilares o hacer un examen del INS en historia y gobierno, ni tomar un juramento de fidelidad a los Estados Unidos.

¡Un consejo! Otra opción para la prueba de la ciudadanía estadounidensa sería solicitar un pasaporte de los Estados Unidos (vea el Capítulo Cuatro). Se utiliza el pasaporte lo más extensamente posible por americanos como prueba de la ciudadanía. Adquirir un pasaporte puede ser más rápido que iniciar la solicitud N-600.

Hijo adoptado o no nativo

En el 30 de octubre, 2000, el Presidente Clinton firmó en ley H.R. 2883, el Acto de Ciudadanía para Niños de 2000. Efectivo el 27 de febrero, 2001, ciertos niños que nacieron en el extranjero, incluyendo niños adoptados, adquieren automáticamente la ciudadanía si se cumplen con los requisitos siguientes:

- El niño tiene a lo menos un padre con la ciudadanía de los Estados Unidos (sea por nacimiento o la naturalización);

- El niño tiene *menos* de 18 años de edad.

- El niño se reside actualmente permanentemente en Los Estados Unidos en la custodia legal y física del padre con la ciudadanía estadounidensa.

- El niño es un residente legal permanente.

- Un niño adoptado cumple con los requisitos aplicables a los niños adoptados bajo la ley de inmigración.

La prueba de la ciudadanía no se admite automáticamente a los niños elegibles. Si se desea la prueba, los padres de los niños elegibles pueden solicitar para un Certificado de la Ciudadanía o un pasaporte.

El Acto de la Ciudadanía para los Niños de 2000 no proporciona a la ciudadanía automática para los niños no nativos o adoptados que residen *fuera* de los Estados Unidos. Para esos niños el padre con ciudadanía estadounidensa *necesitará solicitar la naturalización* a nombre del niño. El proceso de la naturalización no puede ocurrir en el extranjero. El niño necesitará estar en los Estados Unidos temporalmente para completar el trámite de la naturalización y tomar el Juramento de Fidelidad (si tiene suficientes años de edad para comprenderlo). Comuníquese con el INS para más información.

Filing fee waiver

Those applicants who cannot afford the fees associated with naturalization may be eligible for a fee waiver. Generally this entails including an affidavit, or unsworn declaration, with your application that requests the fee waiver and states the specific reasons why you are unable to pay the fee. You will need to include supporting documentation that *proves* your financial situation. Contact the INS for more specifics on requesting a fee waiver.

Mailing your application

Before you mail your application, make a copy of it! It will be a valuable reference in preparation for your interview. And, having a copy will be very helpful in the event your original is lost. In addition, bring your copy along with you when you go for your interview. Because of your application's importance, use "Certified Mail" with "Return Receipt Requested." You will then get confirmation that the INS did, in fact, receive your application. It is best to use a large flat envelope, preferably 9" by 12", for mailing your original N-400 Application and contents. After that comes a wait, sometimes a period of several months. However, the time can be put to good use. Use it to study for the civics test, and even to practice your English, if necessary.

Application for Certificate of Citizenship (N-600)

The other application mentioned at the beginning of this chapter is Form N-600, "Application for Certificate of Citizenship." This one is for people who believe they are already citizens through someone else, such as a parent or spouse, and want to get written proof of their citizenship. The use of this form is absolutely voluntary and does not affect your actual citizenship in any way. File this form only if you personally would like to have a certificate. The INS does not require it, but they provide the form to help you obtain proof that you are a citizen, if you want to do that.

Since you are not applying to become a citizen, you are not required to submit fingerprints or go through an INS examination on history and government nor take an oath of allegiance to the United States.

Quick tip! Another option for proof of U.S. citizenship would be to apply for a U.S. passport instead (see Chapter Four). A U.S. passport is most widely used by Americans as proof of citizenship. Acquiring a U.S. passport may be considerably faster than filing an N-600 application.

Esposo(a) que "adquiere" la ciudadanía

En el pasado era posible que una mujer adquiriera la ciudadanía de los Estados Unidos simplemente casándose con un ciudadano de los Estados Unidos. Eso ya no es posible. Muy pocas, en realidad, se calificarán bajo las reglas anteriores debido a la edad:

1. Si ella estaba casada con el ciudadano antes del 22 de enero de 1922;

o

2. Si ella estaba casada con un Residente Permanente que se convirtió en un ciudadano estadounidense durante el matrimonio o antes del 22 de enero de 1922.

Las circunstancias varían muchos para los que se vuelven ciudadanos por medio de "adquisición." Hay más detalles anotados en el folleto, "Guide to Naturalization," (Un Guía para la Naturalización) Formulario M-476. Si usted todavía no está seguro de haber *adquirido* la ciudadanía, (después de leer el folleto) sería buena idea que solicitara ayuda a un abogado de inmigración o al INS.

Cómo llenar el formulario N-600

Si usted quiere someter un certificado de ciudadanía para usted mismo o para su hijo menor de edad, refiérase a la Muestra 3. También, tiene usted que entregar cualquier documento que pidan para demonstrar su derecho a la ciudadanía por adquisición. Junto con la solicitud N-600, envíe un cheque no reembolsable o giro postal y tres fotografías de color, según lo especificado en la Muestra 2.

Foreign-born children or adopted children

On October 30, 2000, President Clinton signed into law H.R. 2883, the Child Citizenship Act of 2000. Effective February 27, 2001, certain foreign-born children, including adopted children, automatically acquire citizenship if the following requirements are met:

- The child has at least one United States citizen parent (by birth or naturalization);

- The child is *under* 18 years of age;

- The child is currently residing permanently in the United States in the legal and physical custody of the U.S. citizen parent;

- The child is a lawful permanent resident;

- An adopted child meets the requirements applicable to adopted children under immigration law.

Proof of citizenship is not automatically issued to eligible children. If proof is desired, parents of eligible children may apply for a Certificate of Citizenship or a passport.

The Child Citizenship Act of 2000 does not provide automatic citizenship for foreign-born or adopted children residing *outside* the United States. For those children, the U.S. citizen parent will need to *apply for naturalization* on behalf of the child. The naturalization process cannot take place overseas. The child will need to be in the United States temporarily to complete the naturalization processing and take the Oath of Allegiance (if old enough to understand it). Contact the INS for more information.

Spouses who "acquire" citizenship

In the past it was possible for a woman to acquire United States citizenship simply by marrying a U.S. citizen. That is no longer possible. Very few, in fact, will qualify under the old rules due to age:

1. She was married to the citizen before January 22, 1922;

or

2. She was married to a Permanent Resident who became a U.S. citizen during the marriage and before January 22, 1922.

Circumstances vary greatly for those who become citizens through "acquisition." More details are provided in the INS booklet, "A Guide to Naturalization,"

Form M-476. If you are still uncertain (after reading that booklet) whether or not you have *acquired* citizenship, it would be a good idea to seek advice from the INS or an immigration attorney.

How to fill out the Form N-600

If you want to file for a Certificate of Citizenship for yourself or your minor child, refer to Sample 3 in this chapter. You must also submit whatever documents are called for to prove your claim for citizenship by acquisition. Be sure to include a non-refundable check or money order and three, color photographs as specified in Sample 2 with your Form N-600 application.

Sample 3: Form N-600
Application for Certificate of Citizenship (Page 1)

U.S. Department of Justice
Immigration and Naturalization Service

Application for
Certificate of Citizenship

OMB NO. 1115-0018

FEE STAMP

Take or mail this application to:
IMMIGRATION AND NATURALIZATION SERVICE

(Print or type) MARIA ULLOA-CONTRERAS _____ nee _____
(Full, True Name, without Abbreviations)   (Maiden name, if any)

1234 S. STANDARD
(Apartment number, Street address, and if appropriate, "in care of")

SANTA ANA ORANGE CA 92701
(City)   (Country)   (State) (Zip Code)

(714) 862-5555
(Telephone Number)

Date JULY 3, 2001

ALIEN REGISTRATION
NO. NONE

(SEE INSTRUCTIONS. BE SURE YOU UNDERSTAND EACH QUESTION BEFORE YOU ANSWER IT.)

I hereby apply to the Commissioner of Immigration and Naturalization for a certificate showing that I am a citizen of the United States of America.

(1) I was born in MEXICALI, BAJA CALIFORNIA on 04-11-1984
    (City) (State or Country)   (Month) (Day) (Year)

(2) My personal description is: Gender F ; height 5 feet 6 inches;

Marital status: ☑ Single; ☐ Married; ☐ Divorced; ☐ Widow(er).

(3) I arrived in the United States at SAN YSIDRO CALIFORNIA on 09-07-1996
                                      (City and State)   (Month) (Day) (Year)

under the name MARIA ULLOA-CONTRERAS by means of CAR
                                                    (Name of ship or other means of arrival)

☐ on U. S. Passport No. N/A _____ issued to me at _____ on _____
                                                        (Month) (Day) (Year)

☐ on an Immigrant Visa. ☑ Other (specify) BIRTH CERTIFICATE

(4) FILL IN THIS BLOCK ONLY IF YOU ARRIVED IN THE UNITED STATES BEFORE JULY 1, 1924.

(a) My last permanent foreign residence was N/A
                                               (City)   (Country)

(b) I took the ship or other conveyance to the United States at _____
                                                                 (City)   (Country)

(c) I was coming to _____ at _____
                    (Name of person in the United States)   (City and State where this person was living)

(d) I traveled to the United States with _____
                                          (Names of passengers or relatives with whom you traveled, and their relationship to you, if any)

(5) Have you been out of the United States since you first arrived? ☐ Yes ☑ No; If "Yes," fill in the following information for every absence.

DATE DEPARTED	DATE RETURNED	Name of airlines or other means used to return to the United States	Port of return to the United States

(6) I have NOT filed a petition for naturalization. (If "have," attach full explanation.)
      (have) (have not)

TO THE APPLICANT. - Do not write between the double lines below. Continue on next page.

ARRIVAL RECORDS EXAMINED		ARRIVAL RECORD FOUND	
Card index		Place	Date
Index books		Name	
Manifest		Manner	
		Marital status	Age
		(Signature of person making search)	

Form N-600 (Rev. 10/11/00)Y

Form N-600
Application for Certificate of Citizenship (Page 2)

(CONTINUE HERE)

(7) I claim United States citizenship through my *(check whichever applicable)* ☑father; ☐mother; ☐both parents;

☐adoptive parent(s); ☐husband

(8) My father's name is ROBERTO ULLOA ; he was born on 05 - 16 - 1960
(Month) (Day) (Year)

at ANAHEIM CALIFORNIA ; and resides at 551 RIVER RD. CORONA CA
(City) (State or Country) (Street address, city and State or country. If dead, write

He became a citizen of the United States by ☑birth; ☐naturalization on _____
"dead" and date of death.) (Month) (Day) (Year)

in the N/A Certificate of Naturalization No.
(Name of court, city and State)

☐through his parent(s), and _____ issued Certificate of Citizenship No. A or AA _____
(was) (was not)

(If known) His former Alien Registration No. was _____

He has NOT lost United States citizenship. *(If citizenship lost, attach full explanation.)*
(has) (has not)

He resided in the United States from 1960 to 1969 ; from 1989 to present ; from _____ to _____
(Year) (Year) (Year) (Year) (Year) (Year)

from _____ to _____ ; from _____ to _____ ; I am the child of his _____ marriage.
(Year) (Year) (Year) (Year) (1st, 2d, 3d, etc.)

(9) My mother's present name is CAROLINA CONTRERAS-ULLOA ; her maiden name was CAROLINA CONTRERAS-ESPOZA ;

she was born on 12-25-1961 ; at GUADALAJARA JALISCO MEXICO; she resides
(Month) (Day) (Year) (City) (State or country)

at 551 RIVER ROAD CORONA CALIFORNIA . She became a citizen of the
(Street address, city, and State or country. If dead, write "dead" and date of death.)

United States by ☐birth; ☐naturalization under the name of N/A ;

on _____ in the _____
(Month) (Day) (Year) (Name of court, city, and State)

Certificate of Naturalization No. _____ ; ☐through her parent(s), and _____ issued Certificate of
(was) (was not)

Citizenship No. A or AA _____ (If known) Her former Alien Registration No. was _____

She _____ lost United States citizenship. *(If citizenship lost, attach full explanation.)*
(has) (has not)

She resided in the United States from 1996 to present ; from _____ to _____ ; from _____ to _____ ;
(Year) (Year) (Year) (Year) (Year) (Year)

from _____ to _____ ; from _____ to _____ ; I am the child of her 1st marriage.
(Year) (Year) (Year) (Year) (1st, 2d, 3d, etc.)

(10) My mother and my father were married to each other on 06-14-1982 at MEXICALI BAJA CA MEXICO
(Month) (Day) (Year) (City) (State or country)

(11) If claim is through adoptive parent(s):

I was adopted on N/A in the _____
(Month) (Day) (Year) (Name of Court)

at _____ by my _____ who were not United States citizens at that time.
(City or town) (State) (Country) (mother, father, parents)

(12) My N/A served in the Armed Forces of the United States from _____ to _____ and _____
(father) (mother) (Date) (Date) (was) (was not)

honorably discharged.

(13) I have NOT lost my United States citizenship. *(If citizenship lost, attach full explanation.)*
(have) (have not)

(14) I submit the following documents with this application:

Nature of Document	Names of Persons Concerned
BIRTH CERTIFICATE	APPLICANT- (Maria Ulloa-Contreras)
MARRIAGE CERTIFICATE	PARENTS- (Roberto + Carolina Ulloa)
BIRTH CERTIFICATE	FATHER- (Roberto Ulloa)

Form N-600 (Rev. 10/11/00)Y Page 2

Form N-600
Application for Certificate of Citizenship (Page 3)

(15) Fill in this block if your brother, sister, mother or father ever applied to the INS for a certificate of citizenship.

NAME OF RELATIVE	RELATIONSHIP	DATE OF BIRTH	WHEN APPLICATION SUBMITTED	CERTIFICATE NO. AND FILE NO., IF KNOWN, AND LOCATION OF OFFICE

(16) Fill in this block only if you are now or ever have been a married woman. I have been married _____ time(s), as follows:
(1, 2, 3 etc.)

DATE MARRIED	NAME OF HUSBAND	CITIZENSHIP OF HUSBAND	IF MARRIAGE HAS BEEN TERMINATED:	
			Date Marriage Ended	How Marriage Ended (Death or Divorce)

(17) Fill in this block only if you claim citizenship through a husband. *(Marriage must have occurred prior to September 22, 1922.)*

Name of citizen husband ___N/A___ ; he was born on _____
(Give full and complete name)   (Month) (Day) (Year)

at _____ ; and resides at _____ He became a citizen of the
(City) (State or country)   (Street address, city, and State or country. If dead, write "dead" and date of death.)

United States by ☐ birth; ☐ naturalization on _____ in the _____ Certificate of
(Month) (Day) (Year)   (Name of court, city, and state)

Naturalization No. _____ ; ☐ through his parent(s), and _____ issued Certificate of Citizenship No. A or AA
(was) (was not)

_____ . He _____ since lost United States citizenship. *(If citizenship lost, attach full explanation.)*
(has) (has not)

I am of the _____ race. Before my marriage to him, he was married _____ time(s), as follows:
(1,2, 3,etc.)

DATE MARRIED	NAME OF WIFE	IF MARRIAGE HAS BEEN TERMINATED:	
		Date Marriage Ended	How Marriage Ended (Death or Divorce)

(18) Fill in this block only if you claim citizenship through your stepfather. *(Applicable only if mother married U. S. Citizen prior to September 22, 1922.)*

The full name of my stepfather is ___N/A___ ; he was born on _____ at _____ ;
(Month) (Day) (Year)   (City) (State or country)

and resides at _____ He became a citizen of the United States by ☐ birth;
(Street address, city, and State or country. If dead, write "dead" and date of death.)

☐ naturalization on _____ in the _____ Certificate of Naturalization No. _____ ;
(Month) (Day) (Year)   (Name of court, City and State)

☐ through his parent(s), and _____ issued Certificate of Citizenship No. A or AA _____ He _____ since lost United
(was) (was not)   (has) (has not)

States citizenship. *(If citizenship lost, attach full explanation.)* He and my mother were married to each other on _____ at _____
(Month) (Day) (Year)   (City and State or

_____ My mother is of the _____ race. She _____ issued Certificate of Citizenship No. A
country)   (was) (was not)

Before marrying my mother, my stepfather was married _____ time(s), as follows:
(1, 2, 3,etc.)

DATE MARRIED	NAME OF WIFE	IF MARRIAGE HAS BEEN TERMINATED:	
		Date Marriage Ended	How Marriage Ended (Death or Divorce)

(19) I __have NOT__ previously applied for a certificate of citizenship on _____ , at _____
(have) (have not)   (Date)   (Office)

(20) Signature of person preparing form, if other than applicant. I declare that this document was prepared by me at the request of the applicant and is based on all information of which I have any knowledge.

SIGNATURE

ADDRESS:	DATE

(SIGN HERE) *Maria Ulloa-Contreras*
(Signature of applicant or parent or guardian)

Form N-600 (Rev. 10/11/00)Y Page 3

Form N-600
Application for Certificate of Citizenship (Page 4)

APPLICANT. - Do not fill in or sign anything on this page

AFFIDAVIT

I, the _____ , do swear
  (Applicant, parent, guardian)
that I know and understand the contents of this application, signed by me, and
of attached supplementary pages numbered ( ) to ( ), inclusive;
that the same are true to the best of my knowledge and belief; and that
corrections numbered ( ) to ( ) were made by me or at my request.

Subscribed and sworn to before me upon examination of the applicant
(parent, guardian) at _____,
this _____ day of _____, _____
and continued solely for:

_____
(Signature of applicant, parent, guardian) .

_____
(Officer's Signature and Title)

REPORT AND RECOMMENDATION ON APPLICATION

On the basis of the documents, records, and persons examined, and the identification upon personal appearance of the underage beneficiary, I find that
all the facts and conclusions set forth under oath in this application are _____ true and correct; that the applicant did _____ derive or acquire United
States citizenship on _____, through
                      (Month) (Day) (Year)

and that (s)he _____ been expatriated since that time. I recommend that this application be _____ and that
                (has) (has not)   (granted)   (denied)
_____ Certificate of citizenship be _____ issued in the name of _____
(A) (AA)
In addition to the documents listed in Item 14, the following documents and records have been examined:

Person Examined	Address	Relationship to Applicant	Date Testimony Heard
_____	_____	_____	_____
	_____		
_____	_____	_____	_____
	_____		

Supplementary Report(s) No.(s) _____ Attached.

Date _____, _____

_____
(Officer's Signature and Title)

I do _____ concur in the recommendation

Date _____, _____

_____
(Signature of District Director or Officer in Charge)

Form N-600 (Rev. 10/11/00)Y Page 4

Capítulo Tres
La Entrevista y el Examen

Conseguir una cita

Después de entregar su solicitud terminada, el costo, y cualquier documento requerido, puede usted contar con una espera, posiblemente varios meses, antes de que le notifiquen de su cita. Recibirá una notificación escrita por correo del INS que le dirigirá cuando y adonde debe de comparecer para su entrevista.

Guarde la notificación en un lugar seguro, porque el INS no le enviará otra. También es buena idea escribir esta información en la copia que hizo de la Solicitud N-400. Trate de no cambiar la fecha ni la hora de la cita. Hacer eso podía retrasar el proceso por varios meses. En lugar, haga cada esfuerzo posible para comparecer a la hora y al sitio designado en la notificación original.

¡Durante los meses de esperar para recibir su notificación de la cita por el correo, es buena idea prepararse para la entrevista!

¡Importante! Si usted no comparece a su entrevista *y* no le ha comunicado con el INS dentro del plazo de un año desde la fecha de su cita arreglada, se le negarán su solicitud para la naturalización.

Presentarse para la cita

- **Llegue temprano para su cita:** Planee a llegar temprano . . . *antes* de la hora de su entrevista.

- **Traiga consigo a un representante (opcional):** No es necesario traer testigos u otras personas consigo a la entrevista, ya que las oficinas del INS están muy ocupadas. Sin embargo, usted puede traer un representante consigo durante la entrevista *si* ha incluido una "Noticia de la Entrada de Aspecto Como Abogado o Representante," cual es el Formulario G-28 con su Solicitud N-400.

- **Lleve consigo los documentos designados del INS:** ¡Esto es *muy importante!* Si el INS solicitó *documentos adicionales* en la notificación de la cita, *traígalos* a la entrevista.

Chapter Three
The Interview and Test

Getting an appointment

After mailing your completed application and the fee plus any required documents, expect to wait, possibly even several months, to get an appointment. Then, you will receive a written notice in the mail from the INS of when and where to appear for your interview.

Keep this notification in a safe place as the INS will not send you a second one. It is a good idea to also write this information on the copy you kept of your N-400 Application. And, try very hard not to reschedule your appointment for a different date and time. That could delay things for several months. Instead, make every effort possible to appear at the time and place stated on your original notification.

During the months of waiting to receive your appointment notification in the mail, it is a good time to prepare for your interview!

Important! If you do not appear at your interview *and* have not contacted the INS within one year from the date your interview was scheduled, your application for naturalization will be denied.

Appearing for your appointment

- **Arrive early for your appointment:** Plan to arrive early . . . *before* the time of your interview.

- **Bring your representative along (optional):** It is not necessary to bring witnesses or other people with you to the interview, as many INS offices are already crowded. However, you may have a representative with you during the interview *if* you have included a "Notice of Entry of Appearance as Attorney or Representative," which is Form G-28 with your N-400 Application.

- **Take with you INS-requested documents:** This is *very important! If* the INS requested *additional documents* in their appointment letter, *bring them* to the interview.

Tomar la entrevista y el examen

Antes de hacerle preguntas, el funcionario del INS le pondrá bajo juramento para decir la verdad. Luego, esté preparado para contestar preguntas sobre lo siguiente:

- Su historia personal.

- Lugar y duración de residencia.

- Evidencia apoyando su solicitud.

- Buena voluntad de tomar el juramento de fidelidad.

- Su enlace con la Constitución.

- Su reputación.

- Su Solicitud N-400.

Sus respuestas a estas preguntas ayudan al oficial del INS a determinar su elegibilidad y su conocimiento del inglés. Se están probando sus capacidades de la *lectura,* del *discurso* y de la *comprensión* cuando usted lee de su solicitud N-400 y contesta preguntas sobre ella. Así pues, mire con cuidado a esa *copia* de su N-400, que usted hizo antes de enviarla al INS. Esté familiarizado con todo y esté preparado para explicar, con honradez, cualquier diferencia que pudiera existir entre su solicitud y los otros documentos.

¡Importante! La carencia del conocimiento del inglés es a menudo el obstáculo más grande en cumplir con los requisitos educativos.

Aún otra manera en que su inglés puede ser probado está en su capacidad *de escribirlo.*

El oficial del INS puede pedir que usted escriba una o dos frases sencillas tales como las siguientes:

I live in the State of California.

I live in the State of California.

We attend church on Sunday.

We attend church on Sunday.

Taking the interview and test

Before asking you questions, the INS officer places you under oath to tell the truth. Then, be prepared to answer questions about the following:

- Your background.
- Place and length of residence.
- Evidence supporting your application.
- Willingness to take the oath of allegiance.
- Attachment to the Constitution.
- Your character.
- Your N-400 Application.

Your answers to these questions help the INS officer to determine your eligibility and your knowledge of English. Your *reading, speaking,* and *comprehension* abilities are being tested when you read from your N-400 Application and answer questions about it. So, take a good look at that *copy* of your N-400, which you made before mailing it to the INS. Be familiar with everything on it, and be prepared to explain, with honesty, any differences that might exist between your application and other documents.

> **Important!** Lack of knowledge of English is often the biggest stumbling block in meeting the educational requirements.

Still another way in that your English may be tested is on your *writing* ability.

> The INS officer may ask you to write one or two simple sentences such as the following:
>
> I live in the State of California.
>
> *I live in the State of California.*
>
> We attend church on Sunday.
>
> *We attend church on Sunday.*

You listen to the sentence. Then write it down. If those sentences are easy for you now, then fine. You are all set.

Usted escucha la frase. Entonces usted la escribe. Si esas frases son fáciles ahora para usted, entonces muy bien. Usted está todo listo.

Además de tener un buen conocimiento básico de inglés, y cumplir con todos los requisitos para la ciudadanía, debe tener también un conocimiento básico sobre los estudios cívicos, que incluye la historia y el gobierno de los Estados Unidos. "Gobierno" quiere decir básicamente, la Constitución. Leer la Constitución entera, es buena manera de empezar a estudiar. Se aparece en el *Apéndice Cuatro* titulado "La Constitución de los Estados Unidos" en la parte atrás de este libro. Lea toda al menos una vez. No sólo le incrementará su conocimiento y su comprensión, pero también su aprecio del gobierno de Los Estados Unidos. ¡Y qué documento verdaderamente fascinante es! ¡Qué sabiduría tenían los constituyentes!

Luego, para prepararse para su examen de entrevista sobre el gobierno y la historia, querrá repasar las 102 preguntas y respuestas proporcionadas para usted en este capítulo. Repáselas tantas veces como sea necesario, hasta que usted lo sepa todo. ¡Y cuando usted lo hace, puede ser que sepa *más* sobre el gobierno y la historia de los Estados Unidos que algunos nativos nacidos ciudadanos! Pero lo más importante, es que usted esté preparado para pasar la prueba de estudios cívicos para su propia naturalización. Aquí están. Estúdielas cuidadosamente.

102 preguntas sobre la historia y el gobierno de los EE.UU.

Las siguientes preguntas y respuestas pretenden a prepararse para la prueba de la historia y el gobierno de los Estados Unidos. Además pretenden suministrarle una poca de perspicacia adicional sobre datos muy fascinantes de nuestro país. Esto permite un mejor entendimiento y aprecio de los Estados Unidos de América y de cómo se produjo. Es posible que las respuestas que se den parecen ser incompletas o incorrectas. Sin embargo, no importa lo que piense usted de ellas, éstas son las respuestas que espera oír el INS.

Historia antigua de los Estados Unidos

1. ¿Cuándo se descubrió la América y por quién?

En 1492, un Italiano llamado Cristóbal Colón pensó incorrectamente que había llegado al continente asiático o las Indias, pero en realidad, en su lugar, había llegado al Hemisferio Occidental (América del Norte y América del Sur).

2. ¿Quíenes fueron los peregrinos y por qué llegaron a vivir a América?

Vinieron para tener libertad religiosa y llegaron en un buque que se llamaba el "Mayflower."

In addition to having a good knowledge of basic English and meeting all the requirements for citizenship, you also must have a knowledge of civics, which includes both United States history and government. "Government" is, for the most part, the Constitution. Reading through the entire Constitution is an excellent starting point. It appears in *Appendix Four* titled "Constitution of the United States of America" at the back of this book. Read it all the way through at least once. This will add not only to your knowledge and understanding, but it will also add to your appreciation of United States government. And, what a truly fascinating document it is! What wisdom of its makers it shows!

Next, to prepare for your interview test on government and history, you will want to review the 102 questions and answers provided for you in this chapter. Go over them as many times as it takes until you know them all. And, when you do, you just might know *more* about United States government and history than some native-born citizens! But most importantly, you will be prepared to pass the civics test for your own naturalization. Here they are. Study them carefully.

102 study questions on U.S. history and government

The following questions and answers are intended to help you prepare for your test about United States history and government. They are also intended to provide you with a little additional insight into some fascinating highlights of our country. This allows for a better understanding and appreciation of the United States of America and how it came to be. It is possible that an answer given in these questions may seem incomplete or even inaccurate. However, whatever you may think of them, they are the answers expected by the INS.

Early history of the United States

1. When was America discovered and by whom?

In 1492, an Italian by the name of Christopher Columbus mistakenly thought he had reached the Asian mainland or Indies but had, in fact, reached the Western Hemisphere (North and South America) instead.

2. Who were the Pilgrims and why did they come to America to live?

They came for religious freedom on a ship called the Mayflower.

3. What holiday was started by the American colonists?

Thanksgiving, as the story goes, originates from a celebration by the Pilgrims and the Native American Indians together for the bountiful harvest of food. It is a major American holiday celebrated every year on the fourth Thursday of November.

3. ¿Cómo se llama el día festivo comenzado por los primeros colonizadores de América?

El Día de Gracias, como se cuenta, se originó cuando los peregrinos y los indios nativos americanos celebraron juntos una cosecha abundante. Es un día festivo significante que se celebra cada año en el cuarto jueves de noviembre.

4. ¿Dónde se estableció el primer poblado inglés de América?

Se lo estableció en Jamestown, Virginia en el año 1607.

5. ¿Cuántas colonias primero formaron los Estados Unidos?
¿Cuántas puede usted nombrar?

En 1776, habían 13 colonias británicas que se unieron y llegaron a ser los primeros 13 estados de los Estados Unidos de América. Fueron Massachusetts, New Hampshire, Connecticut, Rhode Island, Pennsylvania, New Jersey, New York, Delaware, Virginia, North Carolina, South Carolina, Georgia y Maryland.

6. ¿Cuál fue la causa principal de la disputa entre las colonias y su patria, la Gran Bretaña?

La imposición de impuestos sin representación. Los colonizadores creían que deberían ser tributados por sus propias asambleas (legislatura).

7. ¿Qué fue la Fiesta de Té de Boston?

El Rey y el Parlamento al fin se pusieron de acuerdo para revocar todos los impuestos a los colonizadores con la excepción del que llevaba el té. Cuando la Compañia Británica de la India del Oriente mandó por barco millones de libras de té a la gente de Boston en el año 1773, subieron los barcos y tiraron el té al mar en el puerto de Boston, Massachussetts.

8. ¿Quién dijo, "¡Déme libertad o déme la muerte!"?

Patrick Henry lo dijo cuando habló con la Convención de Virginia en 1775.

9. ¿Qué es la Declaración de Independencia?

Es el documento famoso que anunció al mundo la separación y la independencia de las 13 colonias de la Gran Bretaña/Inglaterra. Estas colonias se hicieron los primeros 13 estados y luego nacieron como los Estados Unidos de América.

4. Where was the first successful English settlement in America?

It was founded in Jamestown, Virginia in 1607.

5. How many colonies first made up the United States? How many can you name?

In 1776, there were 13 British colonies, which joined together and became the first 13 states of the United States of America. They were Massachusetts, New Hampshire, Connecticut, Rhode Island, Pennsylvania, New Jersey, New York, Delaware, Virginia, North Carolina, South Carolina, Georgia and Maryland.

6. What was the main cause of dispute between the colonies and their "mother country," Great Britain?

Taxation without representation. The colonists believed that they should be taxed only by their own assemblies (legislature).

7. What was the Boston Tea Party?

The King and Parliament finally agreed to repeal all of the taxes on the colonists except the one on tea. When The British East India Company shipped millions of pounds of tea to the Bostonians in 1773, they boarded the ships and threw the tea into the harbor at Boston, Massachusetts.

8. Who said, "Give me liberty or give me death!"?

Patrick Henry said this when he addressed the Virginia Convention in 1775.

9. What is the Declaration of Independence?

It is a famous document that announced to the world the separation and independence of the 13 colonies from England/Great Britain. Those colonies became the first 13 states, and the United States of America was born.

10. Who wrote most of the Declaration of Independence?

Thomas Jefferson, a leading member of a committee appointed by the Second Continental Congress, did most of the writing.

11. When do we celebrate our nation's birthday?

July 4, 1776, marks the birth of the United States of America. The Fourth of July, known as Independence Day, is a national holiday, and people in the United States celebrate it every year on July 4.

10. ¿Quién escribió la mayor parte de la Declaración de Independencia?

Thomas Jefferson, un miembro y líder del comité nombrado por el Segundo Congreso Continental, escribió la mayor parte de ella.

11. ¿Cuándo celebramos el cumpleaños de la nación?

El 4 de julio de 1776, marca el nacimiento de los Estados Unidos de América. El Cuatro de Julio, conocido como del Día de la Independencia es un día festivo nacional que la gente de los Estados Unidos celebra cada año.

12. ¿Por qué y cómo se introdujo la esclavitud en América?

Trajeron los primeros africanos a las colonias americanas en 1619 por comerciantes holandeses, quienes los vendieron a los plantadores de Virginia. Los compraron para usar como obreros para sus plantaciones.

13. ¿Cuándo fue la Guerra Civil y cuál fue la causa?

Fue una "Guerra entre los Estados" luchado entre 1861 y 1865 sobre la esclavitud y los derechos de los habitantes del Sur (Estados del Sur) para separarse de la unión. Estas palabras famosas, "Una casa dividida, no puede mantenerse sola," decía Abraham Lincoln.

14. ¿Quién fue el Presidente durante la Guerra Civil?

Abraham Lincoln, o el "Honesto Abe" como lo conocían sus compatriotas, fue presidente durante la Guerra Civil. Fue el Presidente décimosexto de los Estados Unidos.

15. ¿Cuál fue el resultado de la Guerra Civil?

Se revocó la esclavitud en 1863 en los estados que se habían rebelado contra la Unión, con la "Proclamación de Emancipación" de Abraham Lincoln. Entonces en 1865, se añadió a la Constitución la Enmienda 13, que prohibió la esclavitud.

El gobierno de los Estados Unidos

16. ¿Qué forma de gobierno tienen los Estados Unidos?

El gobierno es una "república" o democracia representativa, que la definió Abraham Lincoln como "un gobierno del pueblo, por el pueblo y para el pueblo."

12. When and why was slavery introduced in America?

The first Africans in the American colonies were brought by Dutch traders in 1619 who sold them to Virginia planters. They bought them for laborers on their plantations.

13. When was the Civil War and what was its cause?

It was a "War between the States" fought from 1861 to 1865 over slavery and the rights of Southerners (Southern states) to secede from the union. Famous words, "A house divided against itself cannot stand," were said by Abraham Lincoln.

14. Who was President during the Civil War?

Abraham Lincoln, or "Honest Abe" as he was known to his fellow country-men, was the President during the Civil War. He was the 16th President of the U.S.A.

15. What was the result of the Civil War?

Slavery was abolished in 1863 in the states in rebellion against the Union with Abraham Lincoln's "Emancipation Proclamation." Then in 1865, Amendment 13 was added to the Constitution forbidding slavery.

The government of the United States

16. What is the form of government of the United States?

The government is a "republic," or representative democracy, which was defined by Abraham Lincoln as "a government of the people, by the people, and for the people."

17. There are 3 levels of government. What are they?

They are the federal, state and local levels.

18. How is each of the 50 states governed?

Each state has its own separate government and is governed under its own constitution. A state constitution may not, in any way, conflict with the Constitution of the United States.

19. What do we mean by "national" government?

We mean the government of the country as a whole, as opposed to individual states.

17. Hay 3 *niveles* de gobierno. ¿Cuáles son?

Son el federal, el estatal y el local.

18. ¿Cómo se gobiernan los 50 estados?

Cada estado tiene su gobierno separado y se gobierna bajo su propia constitución. La constitución de un estado no puede estar en conflicto de ninguna manera con la Constitución de los Estados Unidos.

19. ¿Qué queremos decir con el gobierno "nacional"?

Queremos decir el gobierno entero de un país, opuesto a los estados individuales.

20. ¿Se conoce el gobierno nacional por otro nombre?

Sí, se llama el gobierno "federal", que significa que los Estados Unidos es una unión, o federación, de los estados.

21. ¿Cuáles son algunos de los poderes del gobierno nacional?

- Imponer y cobrar impuestos.
- Proveer para la defensa nacional.
- Hacer tratados y conducir relaciones con otros países.
- Reglamentar la inmigración y proveer la naturalización.
- Reglamentar el comercio con las naciones extranjeras y entre los estados.
- Acuñar moneda.
- Imponer y cobrar impuestos federales, como los ingresos y el seguro social.

22. ¿Qué es la Constitución?

La Constitución define la construcción y los poderes del gobierno federal y es "la ley suprema de la tierra."

23. ¿Cuándo fue escrita la Constitución y cuando entró en vigencia?

La Constitución fue escrita en 1787, pero comenzó a funcionar en los Estados Unidos en 1789.

24. ¿Puede cambiarse la Constitución?

Sí, se pueden hacer cambios con adiciones que se llaman "enmiendas."

20. Is the national government called by any other name?

Yes, it is called the "federal" government, which means the United States is a union, or federation, of states.

21. What are some of the powers of the national government?

- Levy and collect taxes.
- Provide for the national defense.
- Make treaties and conduct relations with other countries.
- Regulate immigration and provide for naturalization.
- Regulate commerce with states and foreign countries.
- Coin money.
- Levy and collect federal taxes, such as income tax and social security.

22. What is the Constitution?

The Constitution defines the construction and the powers of the federal government and is the "supreme law of the land."

23. When was the Constitution written and when did it take effect?

The Constitution was written in 1787, but the United States began to function under it in 1789.

24. Can the Constitution be changed?

Yes. Changes can be made by additions called "amendments."

25. How is an amendment made to the Constitution?

Amendments may be proposed by a two-thirds vote of both houses of Congress or by a national convention called by Congress. To become law, amendments must then be approved by the legislatures of three-fourths of the states or by special convention in three-fourths of the states.

26. What is the Bill of Rights?

It is the first 10 amendments to the Constitution. All 10 were approved as a group in 1791.

25. ¿Cómo hace una enmienda a la Constitución?

Las enmiendas pueden ser propuestas por dos terceras partes del voto de ambas Cámaras del Congreso o por una convención nacional convocado por el Congreso. Para volverse ley, las enmiendas deben ser aprobadas por los cuerpos legislativos de tres cuartas partes de los estados o por una convención especial en tres cuartos de los estados.

26. ¿Qué es el "Bill of Rights" (Carta de Derechos)?

Son las primeras 10 enmiendas a la Constitución. Se ratificaron todas las 10 como grupo en 1791.

27. ¿Cuáles son algunos de los más importantes derechos garantizados por la Carta de Derechos ("Bill of Rights")?

La Carta de Derechos ("Bill of Rights") protege la libertad de hablar, la libertad de la prensa, la libertad de la religión, el derecho de reunirse pacíficamente y los derechos de los acusados.

28. ¿Cuáles son algunas de las enmiendas más importantes después de la Carta de Derechos? "Bill of Rights"

#13:   La revocación de la esclavitud.

#14:   Garantizar protección igual de la ley y . . .
Un estado no le puede privar a ninguna persona la vida, la libertad, o la propiedad sin proceso legal.

#19:   Darles a las mujeres el derecho de votar.

#22:   Limitar al Presidente a dos plazos de 4 años en su puesto.

#26:   Bajar la edad mínima para votar a 18 años.

29. ¿Cuántas enmiendas tiene la Constitución?

Desde las primeras 10 que forman la Carta de Derechos o sea el "Bill of Rights," han añadido sólo 17 más desde 1791, constituyendo 27 enmiendas en total.

30. ¿Los derechos de quiénes son garantizados por la Constitución y la Carta de Derechos o sea el "Bill of Rights"?

Todo el mundo — incluyendo los ciudadanos y los que no son ciudadanos que viven en los Estados Unidos. (Hay excepciones. Por ejemplo, se quita el privilegio de votar de las personas condenadas de un delito mayor o sea una "felonía.")

27. What are some very important rights guaranteed by the Bill of Rights?

The Bill of Rights protects our freedom of speech, freedom of the press, freedom of religion, the right to peaceably assemble, and the rights of the accused.

28. What are some of the most important amendments after the Bill of Rights?

#13: Abolished slavery.

#14: Guarantees equal protection of the law and . . .
No state may deprive a person of life, liberty, or property without due process of law.

#19: Gave women the right to vote.

#22: Limited the President to two 4-year terms in office.

#26: Lowered the minimum voting age to 18 years.

29. How many amendments does the Constitution have?

Since the first 10, the Bill of Rights, there have been only 17 more amendments added since 1791, making a total of 27 amendments.

30. Whose rights are guaranteed by the Constitution and the Bill of Rights?

Everyone's — including citizens and non-citizens living in the United States. (There are exceptions. For example, convicted felons have their voting privilege taken away.)

31. The government of the United States is divided into three branches. What are they?

Legislative branch (Congress), which makes the laws.

Executive branch (the President), which enforces the laws.

Judicial branch (courts), which interprets the laws.

The legislative branch

32. What makes up the legislative branch (also known as Congress)?

Congress is made up of two "houses," the House of Representatives and the Senate.

33. What is the purpose of the legislative branch (Congress)?

The legislative branch *makes* the laws.

31. Se divide el gobierno de los Estados Unidos en tres *ramas.* ¿Cuáles son?

La rama legislativa (el Congreso), que hace las leyes.

La rama ejecutiva (el Presidente), que pone en ejecución las leyes.

La rama judicial (los Tribunales), que interpreta las leyes.

La rama legislativa

32. ¿De qué constituye la rama legislativa (conocido como el Congreso)?

Se constituye el Congreso de dos "cámaras," la Cámara de Representantes y el Senado.

33. ¿Cuál es el objeto de la rama legislativa (Congreso)?

La rama legislativa *hace* las leyes.

34. ¿Quién se elige a los miembros del Congreso — o sea, los Senadores y los Representantes?

La gente los elige.

35. ¿Cuántos representantes tiene el Congreso?

Tiene un total de 435. El número de representantes de cada estado se basa en la población de cada estado. (ej. Un representante para aproximadamente cada 600,000 personas en 2001, según los censos de 2000.)

36. ¿Cuáles son las calificaciones mínimas para un representante de la Cámara (Congreso)?

Un representante debe de tener al menos 25 años de edad, ser un ciudadano de los EE.UU. por 7 años al menos, y residir en el estado en el cual él o ella se elige.

37. ¿Cómo se eligen los representantes y por cuánto tiempo?

La gente los elige por un plazo de 2 años.

38. ¿Cuántas veces puede un representante ser reelegido?

No hay límite.

39. ¿Quién preside sobre la Cámara de Representantes?

El Orador de la Cámara, escogido por los Representantes mismos, preside sobre sus sesiones.

34. Who elects the members of Congress — that is, the Senators and the Representatives?

The people elect them.

35. How many representatives are there in Congress?

There are a total of 435. The number of representatives each state has is based on the population of each state (i.e. one representative for approximately every 600,000 people in 2001 per the 2000 census).

36. What are the minimum qualifications for a representative to the House (Congress)?

A representative must be at least 25 years old, a U.S. citizen for at least 7 years, and a resident of the state in which he or she is elected.

37. How are representatives elected and for how long?

The people elect them for a term of 2 years.

38. How many times may a representative be re-elected?

There is no limit.

39. Who presides over the House of Representatives?

The Speaker of the House, chosen by the Representatives themselves, presides over its sessions.

40. How many Senators are there in Congress?

There are 100 senators, two from each state.

41. What are the minimum qualifications of a Senator?

A Senator must be at least 30 years old, at least 9 years a citizen of the U.S.A., and a resident of the state from which he or she is elected.

42. How are Senators elected and for how long?

They are elected by the people for a term of 6 years.

43. How many times may a Senator be re-elected?

There is no limit.

40. ¿Cuántos Senadores hay en el Congreso?

Hay 100 senadores, dos de cada estado.

41. ¿Cuáles son las calificaciones mínimas para un Senador?

Un Senador debe de tener al menos 30 años de edad, al menos 9 años como ciudadano de los EE. UU., y ser un residente en el estado del cual él o ella se elige.

42. ¿Cómo se eligen los Senadores y por cuánto tiempo?

Son elegidos por la gente por un plazo de 6 años.

43. ¿Cuántas veces puede un Senador ser reelegido?

No hay límite.

44. ¿Quién preside sobre el Senado?

El Vice-Presidente es el Presidente del Senado y preside sobre sus sesiones.

45. Nombre los dos Senadores de su estado.

(Por lo general, enumeran a los oficiales gubernativos, incluyendo los senadores de su estado en su libro de teléfono, o a lo mejor, se le puede consultar en la biblioteca pública.)

46. ¿Por qué tiene la Cámara de Representantes 435 representantes y el Senado solamente tiene 100 Senadores?

Se eligen los Representantes según la población de su estado. Así que los estados que tienen una población más grande, cuentan con más representantes, y los estados más chicos, cuentan con menos. Pero en el Senado, cada estado tiene derecho a tener exactamente 2 Senadores, que permite que cada estado, a pesar de su población, tiene representación igual.

47. ¿Cómo se proponen las leyes en el Congreso?

Cada ley federal comienza como un propósito o sea un "bill," el cual es una propuesta presentado por un legislador (un representante o un senador) al Congreso para que se considere y se le tome alguna acción.

44. Who presides over the Senate?

The Vice-President is President of the Senate and presides over its sessions.

45. Name the 2 Senators from your state.

(Government officials, including your state senators are usually listed in a phone book or may be looked up at a public library.)

46. Why does the House of Representatives have 435 representatives and the Senate only 100 Senators?

Representatives are elected according to the population of a state. So, states with more people have more representatives, and smaller states with less people, get fewer representatives. But in the Senate, every state is entitled to exactly 2 senators, which allows every state, regardless of its population, to have equal representation.

47. How are laws proposed in Congress?

Every federal law begins as a "bill" which is a proposal submitted by a legislator (a representative or a senator) to Congress for consideration and action.

48. How does a bill become a law?

A bill may be introduced in either the House or the Senate. If passed in one house, it is sent to the other. If passed again, it is sent to the President to be signed. After the President signs the bill, it becomes a law.

49. Can a bill become a law without the President's signature?

Yes. If the President refuses to sign (this is called a "veto"), the bill must go back to Congress, and if it can be passed by a two-thirds vote in both the House and Senate, it becomes a law. A bill can also become a law if the President does not respond within ten days (unless Congress adjourns within that 10 days).

50. What are some important powers of Congress?

- To levy and collect taxes.
- To regulate trade.
- To provide for coining money and regulating its value.
- To declare war.

48. ¿Cómo se hace ley un propósito o sea un "bill"?

Un propósito se puede presentar ya sea en la Cámara o en el Senado. Si se aprueba en una casa, se manda a la otra. Si se vuelve a aprobar, se manda al Presidente para que él lo firme. Después de que lo firma el Presidente, se hace ley.

49. ¿Puede un propósito o un "bill" hacerse ley sin la firma del Presidente?

Sí. Si el Presidente se niega a firmarlo (ésto se llama un veto) regresa el propósito al Congreso, y si entonces dos terceras partes votan por él en ambos el Senado y la Cámara, se vuelve ley. También un propósito se hace ley si el Presidente no responde dentro de diez días (a menos que se aplaza el Congreso dentro de 10 días).

50. ¿Cuáles son algunos de los poderes importantes del Congreso?

- Imponer y cobrar impuestos.
- Reglamentar el comercio.
- Proveer la acuñación de moneda y reglamentar su valor.
- Declarar guerra.

51. ¿Dónde se reúne el Congreso?

Se reúne en el Capitolio situado en Washington, D.C.

La rama ejecutiva

52. ¿Cuál es el objeto de la rama ejecutiva del gobierno?

La rama ejecutiva *pone en ejecución* las leyes.

53. ¿De qué constituye la rama ejecutiva?

Se constituye del Presidente, del Gabinete y sus Departamentos.

54. ¿Quién es el ejecutivo de más poder?

El Presidente es el ejecutivo de más poder.

55. ¿Quién fue el primer Presidente de los Estados Unidos?

George Washington fue declarado bajo juramento como nuestro primer presidente en 1789.

51. Where does Congress meet?

They meet in the Capitol building in Washington, D.C.

The executive branch

52. What is the purpose of the executive branch of government?

The executive branch *enforces* the laws.

53. What makes up the executive branch of government?

It is made up of the President, the Cabinet and its Departments.

54. Who is the chief executive?

The President of the United States is the chief executive.

55. Who was the first President of the United States?

George Washington was sworn in as our first president in 1789.

56. Where does the President live?

The White House in Washington, D.C. is home to the President.

57. What are the minimum qualifications to be President?

The President of the United States must be at least 35 years old, native-born, and at least 14 years a resident of the United States.

58. How long is the term of office for President of the United States?

A President is elected for 4 years. The 22nd amendment to the Constitution states, "No person shall be elected to the office of the President more than twice . . ." Therefore, a President may serve a maximum of two terms, or 8 years. (A maximum term of *10* years is possible *if* the President was the Vice-President and became President per Amendment #25.)

59. When are elections for President and Vice-President held?

They are held every 4 years in November — on the first Tuesday (after the first Monday) of the month.

56. ¿Dónde vive el Presidente?

La Casa Blanca situada en Washington, D.C. es la residencia del Presidente.

57. ¿Cuáles son las calificaciones mínimas para ser Presidente?

El Presidente de los Estados Unidos debe de tener al menos 35 años de edad, ser nativo estadounidense, y residir por lo menos 14 años en los Estados Unidos.

58. ¿Por cuánto dura en su plazo el Presidente de los Estados Unidos?

Un presidente es elegido por 4 años. La 22a enmienda a la Constitución afirma que, "Ninguna persona puede ser elegida al puesto de Presidente más de dos veces . . ." Por eso, el Presidente puede servir al máximo de dos términos, o 8 años. (Un término de *10* años es posible, *si* el Presidente era el Vice-Presidente y se volvía Presidente por la enmienda #25.)

59. ¿Cuándo se convocan las elecciones para el Presidente y el Vice-Presidente?

Se convocan cada 4 años en noviembre — el martes (después del primer lunes) del mes.

60. ¿Cuándo se inaugura el nuevo Presidente?

El 20 de enero siguiendo las elecciones de noviembre, el nuevo Presidente presta juramento y toma el "Juramento de la Oficina." Esto se llama "El Día de la Inauguración" que es el comienzo oficial del plazo del nuevo presidente.

61. ¿Se elige el Presidente por el voto popular?

No directamente. El Presidente y el Vice-Presidente se eligen por representantes de cada estado que se llaman "electores."

62. ¿Quiénes son los "electores?"

Los electores son hombres y mujeres de cada estado que votan, usando votos que se llaman votos electorales, a nombre de la gente de sus estados, para el Presidente y Vice-presidente.

63. ¿Cuántos electores tiene cada estado?

Cada estado tiene electores que equivalen en número al número total de los representantes y los senadores que cada uno tiene. El grupo entero de los electores se llama "el colegio electoral."

60. When is the new President inaugurated?

On January 20 following the November election, the new President is sworn in and takes the "Oath of Office." This is called "Inauguration Day" which is the official beginning of the new president's term.

61. Is the President elected by popular vote of the people?

Not directly. The President and Vice-President are elected by representatives from each state called "electors."

62. Who are "electors?"

Electors are men and women from each state who cast votes called electoral votes, on behalf of the people of their states, for President and Vice-President.

63. How many electors does each state have?

Each state has electors equal to the combined number of representatives and senators it has. The entire group of electors is called the "electoral college."

64. What is the total number of electoral votes cast for President and Vice-President?

There are currently 538 electoral votes — 435 for the House of Representatives, 100 for the Senators, plus 3 for the District of Columbia. A candidate needs at least 270 electoral votes to win.

65. What are some important duties of the President?

- To enforce federal laws.
- To be Commander-in-Chief of the armed forces.
- To appoint justices of the Supreme Court.
- To appoint cabinet members.
- To make treaties with other nations.
- To grant pardons to persons convicted of crimes in federal courts.

66. Can the President declare war?

No. Only Congress can declare war, but the President can order troops into action without the formal declaration of war.

64. ¿Cuál es el número total de votos electorales para el Presidente y el Vice-Presidente?

Hay actualmente 538 votos electorales, 435 de la Cámara de Representantes, 100 del Senado, y 3 más del Distrito de Columbia. Un candidato necesita tener 270 votos electorales para ganar.

65. ¿Cuáles son algunos deberes importantes del Presidente?

- Poner en ejecución las leyes federales.
- Ser el Comandante-en-Jefe de las fuerzas armadas.
- Nombrar los jueces a la Suprema Corte.
- Nombrar los miembros del Gabinete.
- Hacer tratados con otras naciones.
- Otorgarles perdones a personas convictas de crímenes en las cortes federales.

66. ¿Puede declarar guerra el Presidente?

No. Sólo el Congreso puede declarar guerra, pero el Presidente puede ordenarles a las tropas que entren en acción sin una declaración formal de guerra.

67. ¿Cómo se llama el grupo especial que aconseja al Presidente?

Un grupo de aconsejadores que se llama el Gabinete, aconseja al Presidente. Cada aconsejador es jefe de uno de los departamentos ejecutivos.

68. ¿Cómo se hace una persona miembro del Gabinete?

Los miembros son nombrados por el Presidente con el consejo y el consentimiento del Senado.

69. ¿Nombre algunos de los jefes de departamentos que forman parte del Gabinete?

Algunos son: el Secretario de Estado, el Secretario de Hacienda, el Secretario de Defensa, Ministro de Justicia, el Secretario del Interior, el Secretario de Agricultura, y el Secretario de Transporte.

67. What special group advises the President?

A group of advisors called the Cabinet advises the President. Each advisor heads one of the executive departments.

68. How does a person become a Cabinet member?

Members are appointed by the President with the advice and consent of the Senate.

69. Name some of those department heads who make up the Cabinet.

Some are the Secretary of State, Secretary of the Treasury, Secretary of Defense, the Attorney General, Secretary of the Interior, Secretary of Agriculture, and the Secretary of Transportation.

70. Who takes the President's place if he cannot finish his term?

The Vice-President carries out the duties of the President upon the President's death or removal from office. Next in line after the Vice-President is the Speaker of the House and then the President *pro tempore* (meaning "for the time being") of the Senate.

71. Can the President be removed from his/her term of office?

Yes, by impeachment when it is followed by a trial and conviction.

72. What does "impeachment" mean?

It means an accusation of serious misconduct by a government official in the performance of public duties.

73. Who has the power to impeach a federal official?

Only the House of Representatives has the power to impeach (accuse).

74. Who has the power to try an impeached official?

Only the Senate can try an impeached (accused) federal official.

75. How many Presidents have we had up to and including George W. Bush?

George W. Bush is the *43rd* President of the United States.

76. Who are the President and Vice-President today?

(This information is readily available in newspapers, magazines, libraries and on television.)

70. ¿Quién toma el lugar del Presidente si no termina con su plazo?

El Vice-Presidente lleva al cabo los deberes del Presidente en el caso de la muerte del Presidente,o si se le remueve de su puesto. Después del Vice-Presidente, sigue el Orador de la Cámara y luego el Presidente *pro tempore* (que quiere decir "por temporal") del Senado.

71. ¿Se puede remover el Presidente de su término de cargo?

Sí, por medio de su impugnación, seguida por un juicio y una convicción.

72. ¿Qué quiere decir la "impugnación"?

La impugnación es una acusación de grave mala conducta por un oficial del gobierno en el desempeño de sus deberes públicos.

73. ¿Quién tiene el poder de impugnación sobre un oficial federal?

La Cámara de Representantes solamente tiene el poder de impugnar (acusar).

74. ¿Quién tiene el poder de enjuiciar a un oficial que sea impugnado?

Solamente el Senado puede enjuiciar a un oficial federal que esté impugnado (acusado).

75. ¿Cuántos Presidentes hemos tenido incluyendo a George W. Bush?

George W. Bush es el Presidente *43*.

76. ¿Quiénes son el Presidente y el Vice-Presidente hoy en día?

(Esta información está fácilmente disponible en los periódicos, las revistas, las bibliotecas y en la televisión.)

La rama judicial

77. ¿Cuál es el objeto de la rama Judicial?

La rama judicial *interpreta* las leyes federales.

78. ¿Cuál es el tribunal más alto de los Estados Unidos?

La Suprema Corte es el tribunal más alto del país.

79. ¿Cuál es la ley suprema del país?

La Constitución (y las leyes aprobadas bajo de ella) es la ley suprema del país.

The judicial branch

77. What is the purpose of the judicial branch?

The judicial branch *interprets* the federal laws.

78. What is the highest court in the United States?

The Supreme Court is the highest court of the land.

79. What is the supreme law of the land?

The Constitution (and the laws passed under it) is the supreme law of the land.

80. How many members are there in the Supreme Court?

It has 9 members. One chief justice plus 8 associates sit as a group, hear cases, and decide them by a majority vote.

81. How does a person become a Supreme Court justice and for how long?

Justices are appointed by the President, with the consent of the Senate, for life.

82. Where does the Supreme Court meet?

It meets in the Supreme Court Building in Washington, D.C.

83. When is the Supreme Court in session?

It usually meets from October to June.

84. What is one of the most important duties of the Supreme Court justices?

The justices decide whether laws passed by Congress agree with the Constitution.

85. Does Congress have any power over the Supreme Court?

Yes. Congress determines the number of justices and fixes their pay.

86. Besides the Supreme Court, are there any other Federal courts?

Yes. Congress established a system of lower federal courts, consisting of district courts and circuit courts.

80. ¿Cuántos miembros tiene la Suprema Corte?

Tiene 9 miembros. Un juez principal más 8 asociados se sientan como un grupo para oír casos, y decidirlas por voto de la mayoría.

81. ¿Cómo llega a ser una persona juez de la Corte Suprema y por cuánto tiempo dura su plazo?

Los jueces son nombrados por el Presidente, con el consentimiento del Senado, por vida.

82. ¿Dónde se reúne la Corte Suprema?

Se reúne en el Edificio de la Suprema Corte situada en Washington, D.C.

83. ¿Cuándo está en sesión la Suprema Corte?

Normalmente, se reúne de octubre a junio.

84. ¿Cuál es uno de los más importantes deberes de los jueces de la Suprema Corte?

Los jueces deciden si las leyes aprobadas por el Congreso concuerdan con la Constitución.

85. ¿Tiene el Congreso poder sobre la Suprema Corte?

Sí, el Congreso determina el número de jueces y les fija su sueldo.

86. ¿Además de la Suprema Corte, hay otros tribunales federales?

Sí, el Congreso estableció un sistema de tribunales federales más bajos, que consiste en tribunales del distrito y tribunales superiores.

87. ¿Se le puede remover de su puesto un juez federal?

Sí. Un juez federal puede ser removido solamente por el Congreso—por medio de impugnarlo y condenarlo de crímenes o delitos menores igual que un oficial público.

88. ¿En este momento quién es el Juez Principal de la Suprema Corte?

El Juez Principal William Rehnquist servía en el año 2001. (Se puede encontrar información sobre el Jefe Principal recién nombrado en un almanaque en la biblioteca local.)

87. Can a federal judge be removed from office?

Yes. A federal judge can be removed only by Congress — by being impeached and then convicted of crimes or misdemeanors as a public official.

88. Who is the current Chief Justice of the Supreme Court?

Chief Justice William Rehnquist was serving in the year 2001. (Information on the current Chief Justice may be found in an almanac at your local library.)

Other significant facts

89. What is the national anthem of the United States?

The "Star-Spangled Banner" is our national anthem.

90. Who wrote the Star-Spangled Banner?

Francis Scott Key, inspired by seeing the American flag still flying over Fort McHenry after a British attack, wrote it during the War of 1812.

91. What are the colors of the United States flag and what do they stand for?

The colors are red, white and blue. Red stands for courage, white for truth, and blue for justice.

92. How many stripes are on the flag and what do they mean?

There are 13 stripes that stand for the original 13 states.

93. How many stars are on the flag?

There are 50 stars, each representing one state. The first United States flag had 13 stars, and after that, one star was added each time another state joined the United States.

94. What are the 49th and 50th states?

Alaska is the 49th state and was admitted to the union on January 3, 1959. Hawaii is the 50th state and was admitted on August 21, 1959.

95. Where is the capital of the nation?

Washington, D.C. (District of Columbia), which is *not* a state, is the nation's capital.

Más información significante

89. ¿Qué es nuestro himno nacional?

El "Star-Spangled Banner" (La Bandera Centelleada de Estrellas) es nuestro himno nacional.

90. ¿Quién escribió el "Star Spangled Banner?

Fue escrito durante la Guerra de 1812 por Francis Scott Key, quien fue inspirado al ver la bandera americana todavía ondeando sobre el Fuerte McHenry, después de un ataque británico.

91. ¿Cuáles son los colores de la bandera de los Estados Unidos y qué significan?

Los colores son rojo, blanco y azul. El rojo significa el valor, el blanco significa la verdad, y el azul significa la justicia.

92. ¿Cuántas franjas tiene la bandera y qué significan?

Hay 13 franjas que simbolizan los 13 estados originales.

93. ¿Cuántas estrellas tiene la bandera?

Hay 50 estrellas, cada una representa a un estado. La primera bandera estadounidensa tenía 13 estrellas, y luego se añadía una estrella cada vez que otro estado se unía a los Estados Unidos.

94. ¿Cuáles son los estados 49 y 50?

Alaska es el estado 49 y entró en la unión el 3 de enero, 1959. Hawaii es el estado 50 y entró el 21 de agosto de 1959.

95. ¿Dónde está la capital de la nación?

En Washington D.C. (el Distrito de Columbia), que no es un estado, sino la capital de la nación.

96. ¿Cuáles son los dos partidos políticos mayores?

El partido democrático, con el símbolo del burro, se considera, por lo general, un partido liberal, y

El partido republicano, con el símbolo del elefante, se considera conservador.

96. What are the 2 major political parties?

The Democratic Party, symbolized by the donkey, is generally considered to be liberal, *and*

The Republican Party, symbolized by the elephant, is generally considered to be conservative.

97. Are there any other political parties?

Yes. They are called "third" parties, which usually focus on a single issue (such as the "Green Party" on the environment).

98. What is the most important office in state government?

The governor is the chief executive of the state and is elected by the people of that state.

99. Who is the governor of the state where you live?

(The name of your state governor is usually listed in your telephone directory or may be found at your local library.)

100. What is the capital of the state where you live?

(The name of your state capital is usually clearly marked on most maps. Else, look in an atlas or almanac.)

101. How big is the continental United States?

It is approximately 2,500 miles from the Pacific coast to the Atlantic coast and about 1,300 miles from Mexico to Canada.

102. Give the Pledge of Allegiance:

"I pledge allegiance to the flag

of the United States of America,

and to the Republic for which it stands,

one nation under God, indivisible,

with liberty and justice for all."

97. ¿Hay otros partidos políticos?

Sí. Se les llaman partidos "terceros", cuales se enfocan, por lo general, a una sola causa (como el "Partido Verde" se enfoca al ambiente).

98. ¿Cuál es el puesto más importante del gobierno estatal?

El gobernador es el ejecutivo principal del estado y es elegido por la gente de aquel estado.

99. ¿Quién es el gobernador del estado en que vive usted?

(Por lo general, se enumera el nombre del gobernador de su estado en el libro de teléfono, o se le encuentra en la biblioteca local.)

100. ¿Qué es la capital del estado en que vive usted?

(Por lo general, se marca claramente el nombre de la capital de su estado en la mayoría de los mapas. Si no, busque en un almanaque o un atlas.)

101. ¿Qué tan grandes son los Estados Unidos continentales?

Hay aproximadamente 2,500 millas de la costa pacífica a la costa atlántica y hay 1,300 millas de México a Canadá.

102. Dé usted la Promesa de la Fidelidad:

"Prometo fidelidad a la bandera

de los Estados Unidos de América,

y a la República que representa,

una nación, bajo Dios, indivisible,

con libertad y justicia para todos."

Receiving a decision

The INS can usually *tell* you at the end of your interview if your application for citizenship will be granted or approved. And, the test results are also *written* on a form, such as the one on the following page, by the INS Officer who interviews you.

Now, let's review all the ways in which you may prepare ahead of time to greatly increase your chances of receiving a favorable decision:

- Knowing the answers to the 102 questions,

- Reading through the Constitution in Appendix Four,

- Reviewing the photocopy you made of your N-400 Application for Naturalization (*before* you mailed it),

- Having a good, basic knowledge of the English language, and

- Being honest and of good moral character.

Doing this will prepare you well for successfully passing your interview and tests, thereby qualifying you to have your application for citizenship granted. Next comes the final step in the citizenship process, the Naturalization Oath Ceremony, and what a momentous occasion that will be!

Recibir una decisión

Por lo general, el INS le *indicará* al final de su entrevista, si se va a aprobar o conceder su solcitud para la ciudadanía. También están *estritos* los resultados del examen en el formulario, como aquél que está en la página siguiente, por el Funcionario del INS que le entrevista.

Ahora, repasamos todas las maneras en que usted puede prepararse de antemano para aumentar para usted la probabalidad de recibir una decisión favorable:

- Saber las respuestas a las 102 preguntas,

- Leer la Constitución en el Apéndice Cuatro,

- Repasar la fotocopia que usted hizo de su Solicitud para la Naturalización N-400 (*antes* de que la envió),

- Tener un buen conocimiento básico del idioma inglés, y

- Ser honesto y tener buena reputación moral.

Hacer esto le preparará bien para pasar con éxito su entrevista y pruebas, y de tal modo calificándole para que su solicitud para la ciudadanía sea concedida. Viene después el paso final en el proceso de la ciudadanía, la Ceremonia del Juramento de la Naturalización, y ¡Qué momento especial será!

Sample 4: N-652
Naturalization Interview Results

U.S. Department of Justice
Immigration and Naturalization Service

Naturalization Interview Results

A#: _____

On_____, you were interviewed by INS Officer _____

❑ You passed the tests of English and U.S. history and government.
❑ You passed the test of U.S. history and government and the English language requirement was waived.
❑ The Service has accepted your request for a Disability Exception. You are exempted from the requirement to demonstrate English language ability and/or a knowledge of U.S. history and government.

❑ You will be given another opportunity to be tested on your ability to _____speak / _____read / _____ / write English.
❑ You will be given another opportunity to be tested on your knowledge of U.S. history and government.

❑ Please follow the instructions on the Form N-14.
❑ INS will send you a written decision about your application.

❑ You did not pass the second and final test of your _____ English ability / _____ knowledge of U.S. history and government. You will not be rescheduled for another interview for this N-400. INS will send you a written decision about your application.

A)_____Congratulations! Your application has been recommended for approval. At this time, it appears that you have established your eligibility for naturalization. If final approval is granted, you will be notified when and where to report for the Oath Ceremony.

B)_____A decision cannot yet be made about your application.

It is very important that you:
✓ Notify INS if you change your address.
✓ Come to any scheduled interview.
✓ Submit all requested documents.
✓ Send any questions about this application in writing to the officer named above. Include your full name, A-number, and a copy of this paper.
✓ Go to any oath ceremony that you are scheduled to attend.
✓ Notify INS as soon as possible in writing if you cannot come to any scheduled interview or oath ceremony. Include a copy of this paper and a copy of the scheduling notice.

N-652 (Rev.12/7/99)Y

Capítulo Cuatro
La Ceremonia

Todo lo referente a la Ceremonia de Naturalización

El último paso en el procedimiento de la naturalización es la Ceremonia del Juramento. Es un poco formal, pero breve y sencilla. Desde luego, es muy importante, ya que no es usted ciudadano hasta que tome el Juramento durante la ceremonia.

Después de su Entrevista (y aprobación de su Solicitud), el INS le notificará por correo con la hora, la fecha y el sitio de su Ceremonia del Juramento de la Naturalización. Aquí aparece una muestra de la noticia:

Muestra 5: Formulario N-445A
Aviso de la Ceremonia del Juramento de la Naturalización
(la parte delantera)

U.S. Department of Justice
Immigration and Naturalization Service

OMB #1115-0052
Notice of Naturalization Oath Ceremony

Naturalization and Citizenship Branch

You are hereby notified to appear for a Naturalization Oath Ceremony at the DATE, TIME and PLACE SHOWN BELOW:

Date: _____

Time: _____

Place: _____

You must bring the following with you:
- This letter with ALL of the QUESTIONS ON THE REVERSE side answered in ink.
- Alien Registration Card
- Reentry Permit or Refugee Travel Document.
- Any immigration documents you may have.
- If the naturalization application is ON BEHALF OF YOUR CHILD(ren), BRING your child(ren).

If you cannot come to this ceremony, return this notice immediately and state why you cannot appear. In such case, please use the return address in the extreme upper left hand corner of this letter. You will be sent another notice of ceremony at a later date. You must appear at an oath ceremony to complete the naturalization process.

Chapter Four
The Ceremony

About the Naturalization Ceremony

The last step in the naturalization process is the Oath Ceremony. It is somewhat formal, yet brief and simple. It is, of course, very important, as you are not a citizen until you have taken the Oath during the ceremony.

After your Interview (and approval of your Application), the INS will notify you by mail as to the time, date and place for your Naturalization Oath Ceremony. Here is a sample of the notice:

Sample 5: Form N-445A
Notice of Naturalization Oath Ceremony (front side)

U.S. Department of Justice
Immigration and Naturalization Service

OMB #1115-0052
Notice of Naturalization Oath Ceremony

Naturalization and Citizenship Branch

You are hereby notified to appear for a Naturalization Oath
Ceremony at the DATE, TIME and PLACE SHOWN BELOW:

Date: _____
Time: _____
Place: _____

You must bring the following with you:
- This letter with ALL of the QUESTIONS ON THE REVERSE side answered in ink.
- Alien Registration Card
- Reentry Permit or Refugee Travel Document.
- Any immigration documents you may have.
- If the naturalization application is ON BEHALF OF YOUR CHILD(ren), BRING your child(ren).

If you cannot come to this ceremony, return this notice immediately and state why you cannot appear. In such case, please use the return address in the extreme upper left hand corner of this letter. You will be sent another notice of ceremony at a later date. You must appear at an oath ceremony to complete the naturalization process.

En la *parte trasera* del Formulario N-445A están varias preguntas sobre lo que usted ha hecho desde su entrevista. Llene el dorso de *su* formulario *antes* de ir a la ceremonia.

Formulario N-445A (el dorso)

You should answer these questions the day you are to appear for the naturalization oath ceremony. These questions refer to actions since the date you were first interviewed on your Application for Naturalization. They do not refer to anything that happened before that interview.

After you have answered every question, sign your name and fill in the date and place of signing, and provide your current address.

You must bring this completed questionnaire with you to the oath ceremony, as well as the documents indicated on the front, and give them to the Immigration employee at the oath ceremony. You may be questioned further on your answers at that time.

AFTER THE DATE you were first interviewed on your Application for Naturalization, Form-400:

		ANSWERS	
1.	Have you married, or been widowed, separated, or divorced? (If "Yes" please bring documented proof of marriage, death, separation or divorce).	1. Yes	No
2.	Have you traveled outside the United States?	2. Yes	No
3.	Have you knowingly committed any crime or offense, for which you have not been arrested, or have you been arrested, cited, charged, indicted, convicted, fined, or imprisoned for breaking or violating any law or ordinance, including traffic violations?	3. Yes	No
4.	Have you joined any organization, including the Communist Party, or become associated or connected therewith in any way?	4. Yes	No
5.	Have you claimed exemption from military service?	5. Yes	No
6.	Has there been any change in your willingness to bear arms on behalf of the United States; to perform non-combatant service in the armed forces of the United States; to perform work of national importance under civilian direction, if the law requires it?	6. Yes 7. Yes	No No
7.	Have you practiced polygamy; received income from illegal gambling; been a prostitute; procured anyone for prostitution or been involved in any other unlawful commercialized vice; encouraged or helped any alien to enter the United States illegally; illicitly trafficked in drugs or marihuana; given any false testimony to obtain immigration benefits; or been a habitual drunkard?	1. Yes	No

I certify that each of the answers shown above were made by me or at my direction, & they are true & correct.

Signed at _____ on _____
      (City and State)   (Date)

_____   _____
(Full Signature)   (Full Address and ZIP Code)

Llegue temprano y asegúrese de traer su Tarjeta de Residente Permanente a la ceremonia. Usted la necesitará cuando se inscribe antes de la ceremonia. Actualmente, el INS requiere que entrega su Tarjeta de Residente Permanente cuando se inscribe antes de la ceremonia. No la necesita más porque va a recibir un Certificado de Naturalización, el documento oficial que prueba que usted ahora es ciudadano estadounidense.

On the *back* of the Form N-445A are several questions about what you have done since your interview. Fill out the reverse side of *your* form *before* going to the ceremony.

Form N-445A (reverse side)

You should answer these questions the day you are to appear for the naturalization oath ceremony. These questions refer to actions since the date you were first interviewed on your Application for Naturalization. They do not refer to anything that happened before that interview.

After you have answered every question, sign your name and fill in the date and place of signing, and provide your current address.

You must bring this completed questionnaire with you to the oath ceremony, as well as the documents indicated on the front, and give them to the Immigration employee at the oath ceremony. You may be questioned further on your answers at that time.

AFTER THE DATE you were first interviewed on your Application for Naturalization, Form-400:   **ANSWERS**

1. Have you married, or been widowed, separated, or divorced? (If "Yes" please bring documented proof of marriage, death, separation or divorce).   1. Yes   No

2. Have you traveled outside the United States?   2. Yes   No

3. Have you knowingly committed any crime or offense, for which you have not been arrested, or have you been arrested, cited, charged, indicted, convicted, fined, or imprisoned for breaking or violating any law or ordinance, including traffic violations?   3. Yes   No

4. Have you joined any organization, including the Communist Party, or become associated or connected therewith in any way?   4. Yes   No

5. Have you claimed exemption from military service?   5. Yes   No

6. Has there been any change in your willingness to bear arms on behalf of the United States; to perform non-combatant service in the armed forces of the United States; to perform work of national importance under civilian direction, if the law requires it?   6. Yes   No
     7. Yes   No

7. Have you practiced polygamy; received income from illegal gambling; been a prostitute; procured anyone for prostitution or been involved in any other unlawful commercialized vice; encouraged or helped any alien to enter the United States illegally; illicitly trafficked in drugs or marihuana; given any false testimony to obtain immigration benefits; or been a habitual drunkard?   1. Yes   No

I certify that each of the answers shown above were made by me or at my direction, & they are true & correct.

Signed at _____   on _____

(City and State)   (Date)

_____   _____
(Full Signature)   (Full Address and ZIP Code)

Arrive early and be sure to bring your Permanent Resident Card with you to the ceremony. You will need it when you check in before the ceremony. In fact, the INS requires you to return your Permanent Resident Card when you check in before the ceremony. You won't need it anymore because you will be receiving your Certificate of Naturalization, the official document that proves you are now a United States citizen.

A veces, el INS le da la oportunidad para tomar el juramento el mismo día de la entrevista. Si usted decide hacer eso, le pedirán regresar a la oficina más tarde del mismo día para tomar el Juramento y recibir su Certificado de Naturalización.

Todo lo referente al Juramento de Fidelidad

Lo que sigue es el Juramento de Fidelidad que usted toma durante la ceremonia. Un oficial le leerá cada parte despacio, y usted le repetirá las palabras al oficial.

El Juramento de Fidelidad

Con ésto declaro, bajo juramento,

que yo absolutamente y enteramente renuncio y abjuro toda fidelidad y fe en cualquier príncipe extranjero, potentado, o estado o soberano del cual y al cual hasta ahora he sido súbdito o ciudadano;

que respaldaré y defenderé la Constitución de los Estados Unidos de América contra todo enemigo extranjero o doméstico;

que tendré fe verdadera y fidelidad al mismo;

que portaré armas a nombre de los Estados Unidos cuando se exija por ley;

que prestaré servicios no combatientes a las Fuerzas Armadas de los Estados Unidos cuando se me exija por ley;

que realizaré el trabajo de importancia nacional bajo la dirección civil cuando se requiera la ley; y

que tomo esta obligación libremente sin reserva mental de ninguna clase o al propósito de evasión; así me ayude Dios.

En palabras sencillas, el Juramento quiere decir:

Juro que yo renuncio completamente mi lealtad al país y su gobierno del cual he sido hasta ahora ciudadano o súbdito. Doy toda mi lealtad y apoyo a la Constitución y leyes de los Estados Unidos, y las obedeceré. Si me llaman, lucharé por los Estados Unidos en sus Fuerzas Armadas o desempeñaré todo deber que me requiera la ley. Estoy tomando este juramento de mi propia voluntad sin intención de engañar. Así lo juro ante Dios.

Sometimes, the INS is able to give you the choice of taking the oath on the very same day as your interview. If you decide to do that, you will be asked to return to the office later that day to take the Oath and receive your Certificate of Naturalization.

About the Oath of Allegiance

Following is the Oath of Allegiance that you will take during the ceremony. An official will read each part slowly, and you will repeat the words back to the official.

The Oath of Allegiance

I hereby declare, on oath,

that I absolutely and entirely renounce and abjure all allegiance and fidelity to any foreign prince, potentate, state, or sovereignty, of whom or which I have heretofore been a subject or citizen;

that I will support and defend the Constitution and the laws of the United State of America against all enemies, foreign and domestic;

that I will bear true faith and allegiance to the same;

that I will bear arms on behalf of the United States when required by the law;

that I will perform noncombatant service in the Armed Forces of the United States when required by the law;

that I will perform work of national importance under civilian direction when required by the law; and

that I take this obligation freely, without any mental reservation or purpose of evasion; so help me God.

More simply stated, the Oath means...

I swear that I give up completely all loyalty to the country and government of which I was, up to this time, a citizen or a subject. I will give my full loyalty and support to the Constitution and laws of the United States, and I will obey them. If called upon, I will fight for the United States in its Armed Forces or perform other duties as required by law. I am taking this oath of my own free will and without intent to deceive. I swear or affirm this before God.

Todo lo referente del Certificado de Naturalización

Cuando usted recibe el Certificado de Naturalización, se recomienda que anote la información que lleva en un pedazo del papel y la guarde en un lugar seguro. Es un delito federal hacer fotocopia de él. (¡Por esta razón no tenemos copia de uno apareciendo en este libro!) Algunos ciudadanos recién naturalizados lo emarcan orgullosamente el certificado original para exhibición o para colgar en la pared.

Si su Certificado de Naturalización se pierde, se destruye, o si su nombre se cambia por orden judicial o por matrimonio, usted querrá un certificado nuevo. Después de todo, es su prueba de ser ciudadano estadounidense. Para conseguir uno nuevo, use el Formulario N-565, Solicitud para el Reemplazo del Documento de Ciudadanía.

Todo lo referente al pasaporte Estadounidense

No sólo es el pasaporte estadounidense un beneficio maravilloso de los Estados Unidos, sino también puede ser utilizado como *prueba de la ciudadanía.* Por eso, se le recomienda obtener un pasaporte inmediatamente después de tener su ceremonia de juramento de naturalización. Es más fácil llevarlo con usted mismo que el Certificado de Naturalización. Y, si se pierde el certificado, puede durar mucho tiempo para reemplazarlo. Entretanto, mientras espera, y espera, para recibir un certificado nuevo, ¿cómo proveería evidencia de su ciudadanía estadounidensa si no tuviera el pasaporte? Otra vez, es muy sabio *solicitar su pasaporte inmediatamente* después de volverse ciudadano.

En la página siguiente hay un recado especial para usted, el ciudadano recién naturalizado, de la Oficina de Asuntos Consulares con respecto a la adquisición de un pasaporte estadounidense. Se incluyen datos adicionales y más información detallada, como números de telefóno, direcciones, y una muestra de una solicitud para un pasaporte, en el capítulo que sigue, "Al Fin—La Ciudadanía Estadounidensa."

> **Of interest!** If your religious training or beliefs prevent you from using certain words or phrases in the Oath and if you can provide enough evidence of your reasons to the INS, they may allow you to substitute different words or phrases when you take the Oath.

About the Certificate of Naturalization

When you get your Certificate of Naturalization, it is advisable to write down the information from it on a piece of paper and keep it in a safe place. It is a federal offense to make a copy of it. (That's why no copy of one appears in this book!) Some proud newly naturalized citizens even frame the original certificate for display or hanging on a wall.

If your Certificate of Naturalization is lost or destroyed, or if your name is changed by court order or marriage, you will want to get a new certificate. After all, it is your proof that you are a U.S. citizen. To obtain a new one, use Form N-565, Application for Replacement of Citizenship Document.

About a U.S. passport

Not only is a U.S. passport a wonderful benefit of U.S. citizenship, but it also is used as *proof of citizenship.* That is why you are urged to obtain a U.S. passport immediately after your naturalization oath ceremony. It is easier to carry with you than your Certificate of Naturalization. And, if you lose your certificate, it could take a long time to get it replaced. In the meantime, while you wait, and wait, to get your new certificate, how would you prove U.S. citizenship if you didn't have a

passport? Again, it is wisest to *apply for your passport right away* after becoming a citizen.

On the following page is a special message to you, the newly naturalized citizen, from the Bureau of Consular Affairs regarding obtaining a U.S. passport. Additional facts as well as more detailed passport information, such as phone numbers, addresses, and a sample passport application are included in the next chapter, "United States Citizenship at Last."

M-384
9-85

Passport Services BUREAU OF CONSULAR AFFAIRS
U.S. DEPARTMENT OF STATE
WASHINGTON, D.C. 20524

NOTICE TO NEWLY NATURALIZED CITIZENS REGARDING PASSPORTS

The Office of Passport Services of the Department of State congratulates you on your newly acquired United States citizenship.

One privilege your citizenship entitles you to is a United States passport. The passport is an official document attesting to your citizenship and identifying you for purposes of international travel. It is also official evidence that you are entitled to the protection of the United States Government while you are abroad.

Many naturalized citizens frequently travel abroad to visit relatives and the land of their birth. There have been some unfortunate instances in which citizens were not able to complete emergency travel of a business or family nature because there was not sufficient time to obtain a United States passport. If you are planning to travel, therefore, the Office of Passport Services urges you to apply for and maintain a valid passport at all times.

Applying for your first passport is easy, requiring only a completed application, your naturalization certificate, two recent identical photographs, and appropriate fees. All passport requirements are detailed in the brochure "Your Trip Abroad" available at many Federal and State courts and post offices and at the passport agencies listed on the back of this notice.

Once you have a United States passport, keep it in a safe place where you can get at it quickly when you need it. The loss of a passport is a serious matter which may cause you difficulties. Avoid this problem by safeguarding your passport as you would any valuable possession.

Capítulo Cinco
¡Al Fin — La Ciudadania Estadounidensa!

La ciudadanía estadounidensa es un privilegio y una responsabilidad. Entre los grandes beneficios son la elegibilidad de obtener un pasaporte y el privilegio de votar. Vamos a mirar aquellos, uno por uno.

El pasaporte

Su pasaporte sirve como prueba de la ciudadanía estadounidensa, por lo cual es razón suficiente para desear obtenerle uno enseguida después de su ceremonia de la naturalización. Otra razón buena para tener un pasaporte válido en mano, es si tiene parientes que viven en el extranjero y allí pasa alguna emergencia que requiera su presencia. También, el pasaporte de los EE.UU. permite que usted vaya al Cónsul de los EE.UU. para asistencia en cualquier país que visite. Todas éstas son muy buenas razones para obtener pasaporte tan pronto como se hace ciudadano.

Solicitar un pasaporte estadounidense

¡En primer lugar, un ciudadano que nunca ha tenido un pasaporte estadounidense *necesita hacer solicitud en persona!* Se puede conseguir la solicitud en cualquiera de las 4,500 agencias para el servicio del pasaporte ubicadas por toda la nación — incluyendo muchos correos, bibliotecas, tribunales, un número de oficinas municipales o del condado, y en línea también. ¡Es posible que estén disponibles en su ceremonia de juramento! Llene su solicitud como la muestra en la pagina 103, pero *no lo firme* hasta que se le instruyan.

Chapter Five
U.S. Citizenship At Last!

Being a citizen of the United States is both a privilege and a responsibility. Among the biggest benefits are the eligibility to obtain a U.S. Passport and the privilege to vote. Let's take a look at these, one by one.

Passports

Your passport serves as proof of U.S. citizenship, which is reason enough to want to obtain one right away after your naturalization ceremony. Another good reason to have a valid passport on hand is if you have relatives living overseas and there is an emergency requiring your presence. Also, your U.S. passport allows you to go to the U.S. Consul for help or assistance in the country you are visiting. These are all very good reasons for obtaining your passport as soon as you become a citizen.

How to apply for a U.S. passport

For starters, a citizen who has never before had a U.S. passport must apply in person! A passport application may be obtained at any one of more than 4,500 passport acceptance facilities nationwide — including many post offices, libraries, courthouses, a number of county and city offices, and also on line. They may even be available at your oath ceremony! Complete your application like in the sample on page 103, but do not sign it until instructed to do so.

Que se acompaña la solicitud

Necesita tener lo siguiente cuando vaya en persona a solicitar un pasaporte:

Prueba de la ciudadanía estadounidensa	Certificado de Naturalización Certificado de Ciudadanía Copia certificada del certificado de nacimiento Pasaporte previo de los EE. UU.
Dos fotografías	Dos fotos identícos de color o blanco y negro Tamaño 2″ × 2″ desde la barbilla hasta toda la cabeza La cara entera
Prueba de la Identidad	Certificado de Naturalización Licencia válida de manejar Cartilla militar Pasaporte previo
Costo	El costo depende de la edad
Número de Seguridad Social	Requerido por el Servicio de Rentas Interiores

Si no tiene alguno de los documentos requeridos, comuníquese con un agente de servicios de pasaporte local para averiguar lo que pueda usar en su lugar. Después de entregar la solicitud terminada, tomará entre 5 a 6 semanas para recibirlo por correo.

Necesidad urgente para el pasaporte

En los casos de *necesidad urgente* solamente, llame "la Agencia de Pasaporte." Por lo general, se considera la necesidad urgente un viaje en 14 días o menos. Hay solamente 13 agencias de pasaportes en la nación, y cuando exista una emergencia, usted puede ir a unas de estas oficinas. Primero, necesita llamar y hacer cita. Luego, cuando en persona entrega su solicitud terminada de pasaporte, asegúrese de que ha incluido en ella la fecha de su salida, y sus planes de viajar en la Sección 20. También asegúrese de *llevar con usted la prueba* de sus planes de viajar, como los boletos o el itinerario generado por la línea aérea.

Por un *costo adicional*, la Agencia de Pasaporte tiene disponible un "*servicio acelerado*" donde el pasaporte puede ser procesado dentro de *3 días de trabajo* después de que la agencia haya recibido su solicitud terminada y la otra documentación requerida. Véase el *Apéndice Tres* para una lista de las 13 Agencias de Pasaporte, incluyendo las direcciones y los números de teléfono.

Sample 6: Passport Application

U.S. Department of State

APPLICATION FOR ☐ U.S. PASSPORT ☐ REGISTRATION
(Type or print all capital letters in blue or black ink in white areas only)

1. NAME (First and Middle)
MARIA

LAST
ULLOA-CONTRERAS

2. MAIL PASSPORT TO: STREET / RFD # OR P.O. BOX APT. #
1234 STANDARD STREET

CITY STATE
ORANGE CA

☐ 5 Yr. ☐ 10 Yr. Issue Date _____
☐ R ☐ D ☐ O ☐ DP
End. # _____ Exp. _____

ZIP CODE 92701 **COUNTRY / IN CARE OF (if applicable)** USA

3. SEX ☐ M ☒ F
4. PLACE OF BIRTH (City & State or City & Country) MEXICALI BAJA CALIF
5. DATE OF BIRTH Month Day Year 04/11/1980
6. SOCIAL SECURITY NUMBER (SEE FEDERAL TAX LAW NOTICE ON PAGE 4) 123456789

7. HEIGHT First Inches 5 6
8. HAIR COLOR BLACK
9. EYE COLOR GREEN
10. HOME TELEPHONE 714 862-5555
11. BUSINESS TELEPHONE 714 546-1122
12. OCCUPATION Dental Assistant

13. PERMANENT ADDRESS (DO NOT LIST P.O. BOX) STREET/R.F.D. #   CITY   STATE   ZIP CODE
1234 STANDARD STREET ORANGE CA 92701

14. FATHER'S FULL NAME Last First ULLOA ROBERTO
BIRTHPLACE USA
BIRTHDATE 05/16/56
U.S. CITIZEN ☒ Yes ☐ No
15. MOTHER'S FULL MAIDEN NAME Last First CONTRERAS CAROLINA
BIRTHPLACE Mexico
BIRTHDATE 12/25/57
U.S. CITIZEN ☐ Yes ☒ No

16. HAVE YOU EVER BEEN MARRIED? ☐ Yes ☒ No
SPOUSE'S OR FORMER SPOUSE'S FULL NAME AT BIRTH N/A
BIRTHPLACE
BIRTHDATE
U.S. CITIZEN ☐ Yes ☐ No

DATE OF MOST RECENT MARRIAGE Month Day Year N/A
WIDOWED/DIVORCED? ☐ Yes Give Date ☐ No Month Day Year
17. OTHER NAMES YOU HAVE USED (1) (2)

18. HAVE YOU EVER BEEN ISSUED A U.S. PASSPORT? ☐ Yes ☒ No IF YES, COMPLETE NEXT LINE AND SUBMIT PASSPORT IF AVAILABLE.
NAME IN WHICH ISSUED
MOST RECENT PASSPORT NUMBER
APPROXIMATE ISSUE DATE Month Day Year
DISPOSITION ☐ Submitted ☐ Stolen ☐ Lost ☐ Other

It is necessary to submit a statement with an application for a new passport when a previous valid or potentially valid passport cannot be presented. The statement must set forth in detail why the previous passport cannot be presented. Use Form DS-64.

19. EMERGENCY CONTACT. If you wish, you may supply the name, address and telephone number of a person not traveling with you to be contacted in case of emergency.
NAME ROBERTO ULLOA
STREET 551 RIVER ROAD
CITY CORONA **STATE** CA **ZIP CODE** 92713 **TELEPHONE** 714 567-1313

20. TRAVEL PLANS (not mandatory) Month Day Year
Date of Trip
Length of Trip
COUNTRIES TO BE VISITED:

SUBMIT TWO RECENT IDENTICAL PHOTOS
FROM 1" TO 1-3/8"
2" x 2"
STAPLE

21. STOP. DO NOT SIGN APPLICATION UNTIL REQUESTED TO DO SO BY PERSON ADMINISTERING OATH.
I have not, since acquiring United States citizenship, performed any of the acts listed under "Acts or Conditions" on the reverse of this application form (unless explanatory statement is attached). I solemnly swear (or affirm) that the statements made on this application are true and the photograph attached is a true likeness of me.

X _____ Applicant's Signature - age 14 or older
X _____ Father's/Legal Guardian's Signature (if identifying minor)
X _____ Mother's/Legal Guardian's Signature (if identifying minor)

22. FOR ACCEPTANCE AGENT'S USE
Subscribed and sworn to (affirmed) before me Month Day Year (SEAL)
(Signature of person authorized to accept application)
☐ Clerk of Court; Location _____
☐ PASSPORT Agent
☐ Postal Employee
☐ (Vice) Consul USA

23a. Applicant's or Father's Identifying Documents
☐ Driver's License ☐ Passport ☐ Other (Specify) _____
Issue Date: _____ Expiration Date: _____ Place of Issue: _____
Name _____ ID No. _____

23b. Mother's Identifying Documents
☐ Driver's License ☐ Passport ☐ Other (Specify) _____
Issue Date: _____ Expiration Date: _____ Place of Issue: _____
Name _____ ID No. _____

24. FOR ISSUING OFFICE USE ONLY (Applicant's evidence of citizenship)
☐ Birth Certificate ☐ SR ☐ CR ☐ City Filed/Issued:
☐ Passport Bearer's Name:
☐ Report of Birth:
☐ Naturalization/Citizenship Cert. No: Issued:
☐ Other:
☐ Seen & Returned:
☐ Attached:
APPLICATION APPROVAL

25.
FEE _____ EXEC. _____ EF _____ OTHER _____

DS-11   OMB No. 1405-0004 Expires: 12/31/2001 Estimated Burden - 20 Minutes   Page 3 of 4

Una vez que obtiene su nuevo pasaporte estadounidense, será válido por 5 o 10 años, según su edad de acuerdo con la tabla siguiente:

Si cumplió (vea la edad abajo) cuando el pasaporte fue expedido:	Luego es válido su pasaporte por:
16 años o más	10 años
15 años o menos	5 años

Buen consejo acerca del pasaporte

Aquí hay algunos buenos consejos sobre el viajar y su pasaporte nuevo.

1. Si usted no tiene ningún pasaporte todavía pero ha hecho planes de viajar, de todos modos, solicite el pasaporte enseguida. ¡No espere hasta que se le acerque el día de su salida! Si es posible, debe hacerlo meses, o semanas, por adelantado, para obtener su pasaporte estadounidense.

2. Llene la página de información de emergencia de su pasaporte.

3. Haga 2 copias de la página de identificación del pasaporte. Lleve una copia en un lugar separado del pasaporte. Deje la otra con un pariente o amigo. (Podrían enviarla por telefax a usted)

4. Deje atrás una copia de su itinerario, también, con parientes o amigos para que se le puedan comunicar en el caso de alguna emergencia.

5. Lleve con usted dos fotos adicionales de talla-pasaporte.

6. Notifique la embajada de los EE.UU. o el consulado por teléfono o en persona al llegar a una área remota o un país que sufre problemas civiles.

7. Si tiene alguna dificultad, póngase en contacto con la oficina Consular local de los EE. UU.

What accompanies the application

You will need the to have the following with your application when you go in person to apply for your passport:

Proof of U.S. citizenship	Certificate of Naturalization Certificate of Citizenship Certified copy of birth certificate Previous U.S. passport
Two photographs	2 identical pictures, color or black and white Size: 2″ × 2″ bottom of chin to top of head Full face view
Proof of identity	Certificate of Naturalization Valid driver's license Military ID Previous passport
Fee	Amount varies by age
Social Security number	Required by the Internal Revenue Service

If you do not have one of the required documents, contact your local passport acceptance agent to find out what may be used in its place. After submitting your complete application, it will take up to 5 or 6 weeks to receive your passport by mail.

Urgent need for passport

In cases of *urgent need* only, call the nearest "Passport Agency." Urgent need is usually considered to be travel in 14 days or less. There are just 13 passport agencies in the nation, and in an emergency, go to one of those offices. First, call to see if you need an appointment. Then, when you go in person to submit your completed passport application, be sure you have included your departure date and travel plans on it in Section #20. Also, be sure to *take with you proof* of your travel plans, such as your tickets or airline-generated itinerary.

For an *additional fee,* the Passport Agency has an *"expedited service"* available where a passport can be processed in about *3 working days* from the day the agency gets your completed application and the other required documentation. See *Appendix Three* for a listing of the 13 Passport Agencies including their addresses and phone numbers.

Para más información

Dos recursos excelentes para información sobre el pasaporte son:

El Centro Nacional de Información del Pasaporte (NPIC) que se puede llamar *por un costo:*

1-900-225-5674

o

Su computadora personal en el siguiente sitio del Internet:

http://travel.state.gov/passport_services.html

La votación

La votación es un deber y un derecho sumamente importante. En realidad, es la manera en que preservamos la forma democrática de nuestro gobierno. Una vez dijo Franklin D. Roosevelt que la única manera de garantizar nuestra libertad es por tener un gobierno de suficiente poder para proteger los intereses de toda la gente, y por tener la gente suficiente fuerte y bien informada para mantener el control sobre su gobierno. ¿Hay mejor manera de ejercer control que su voto? Su voto sí cuenta y hace una diferencia. Pues, sabía usted que:

En 1776: *Un voto* le dió a América el idioma inglés en vez del alemán.

En 1845: *Un voto* dejó entrar el Estado de Tejas a la Unión.

En 1876: *Un voto* salvó al Presidente Andrew Johnson de ser despedido de su puesto de la Presidencia.

En 1923: *Un voto* le dió a Adolph Hitler el poder del Partido Nazi.

En 2000: *Solo 537 votos* de aproximadamente 6 millones votos del estado de Florida le dió a George W. Bush la Presidencia de los Estados Unidos.

Fue John F. Kennedy, nuestro presidente 35, quien dijo en su discurso de inauguración:

". . . no preguntes qué es lo que tu país puede hacer por ti, pregunta qué es lo que tu puedes hacer por tu país."

Once you have obtained your new U.S. passport, it will be valid for 5 or 10 years depending on your age in accordance with the following chart:

If you were (see age below) when the passport was issued:	Then your passport is valid for:
16 or older	10 years
15 or younger	5 years

Good advice about passports

Here are a few helpful hints about travel and your new passport:

1. If you have no passport yet but have made travel plans, by all means, apply for your passport right away. Do not wait until your departure time nears! Allow as many months, or weeks, as possible in advance for obtaining your U.S. passport.

2. Fill in the emergency information page of your passport.

3. Make 2 copies of your passport identification page. Carry one copy in a separate place from your passport. Leave the other copy behind with a relative or friend. (They could fax it to you).

4. Leave behind a copy of your itinerary, also, with family or friends so that you can be contacted in case of an emergency.

5. Carry 2 extra passport-size photos with you.

6. Notify the U.S. embassy or consulate by phone or in person upon your arrival in a remote area or in a country experiencing civil unrest.

7. If you get into trouble, contact the local office of the U.S. Consular Service.

¿Qué puede *hacer* usted para su país? *¡Llegue a ser bien informado y luego vote!* Hoy en día es fácil llegar a ser bien informado por medio de la televisión, la radio, los periódicos, las revistas, y aun el internet.

Los ciudadanos bien informados conocen lo que sucede en su comunidad, en su nación, y alrededor del mundo. Aprenden acerca de los candidatos que se postulan. Se basan su opinión sobre los hechos y luego deciden quien puede ser el candidato mejor calificado, y lo que es mejor para su comunidad, estado y país. Thomas Jefferson, el tercer Presidente de nuestro país, lo reconoció cuando él escribió:

> ". . . cuando las cosas llegan al punto de estar tan mal encarriladas que se les llama la atención, se puede contar con la gente, para arreglarlas."

¿Cuál otra manera de convertir las cosas "incorrectas" en cosas "correctas" que por el votar? Además, por supuesto, usted puede expresar su opinión escribiendo a su miembro de Congreso, o al editor de un periódico local.

Empadronarse para votar

Para votar, primero necesita empadronarse. Ya que hay ciertos requisitos de tiempo (a veces 29 días antes de una elección), es buena idea estar preparado por empadronarse tan pronto como se haga ciudadano. Empadrónese en la comunidad en donde vive usted. Si se muda, debe empadronarse otra vez en su nueva comunidad. Para empadronarse, debe usted:

- Ser un ciudadano de los Estados Unidos.

- Ser un residente del estado o la comunidad donde usted vota.

- Tener por lo menos 18 años de edad antes del día de la elección.

- No estar encarcelado o en la probación por la convicción de una felonía.

Empadronarse es un procedimiento sencillo y toma solamente unos cuantos minutos. Sólo se necesita llenar una tarjeta de registro del votante de manera parecida a la muestra en la página 113.

Se puede obtener en persona una tarjeta de Registro de Votante en tales lugares como la biblioteca, el correo, el ayuntamiento, y el Departamento de Vehículos y Motores. Simplemente, envíelo. O, puede visitar la Oficina de Registro de Votante en persona. Se puede obtener el número de teléfono del Registrador de Votante en su comunidad del asistencia telefónica o al principio del libro de teléfono bajo "gobierno."

For additional information

Two excellent sources for additional information about passports are:

The National Passport Information Center (NPIC), which may be reached *for a fee* by calling:

1-900-225-5674

or

Your personal computer at the following internet website:

http://travel.state.gov/passport_services.html

Voting

Voting is an extremely important right and duty. In fact, it is the way we preserve the democratic form of government. Franklin D. Roosevelt once said that the only way to guarantee our liberty is to have a government strong enough to protect the interests of all the people, and to have the people strong enough and well enough informed to maintain control over their government. How better to have control than by your vote? It does count and does make a difference. Why, did you know that:

In 1776: *One vote* gave America the English language instead of German.

In 1845: *One vote* brought the State of Texas into the Union.

In 1876: *One vote* saved President Andrew Johnson from being dismissed from the Office of the Presidency.

In 1923: *One vote* gave Adolph Hitler leadership of the Nazi Party.

In 2000: *Only 537 votes* out of approximately 6 million Florida state votes gave George W. Bush the Presidency of the United States.

It was John F. Kennedy, our country's 35th President, who said during his inauguration:

"... ask not what your country can do for you — ask what you can do for your country."

La tarjeta puede variar un poco de comuinidad a comunidad, pero básicamente, todas requieren la misma información. Asegúrese de marcar su afiliación de "partido político, en el cual tiene confianza. Si no lo sabe o si no quiere usted que sepa nadie, esté seguro de marcar donde dice "Decline to state" (rehuso declararlo). Es su privilegio así hacerlo. Sólo no deje nada en blanco. ¡Marque algo! De otra manera, puede ser que su tarjeta se le considere incompleta y no se le registre.

El votar popular comparado con el electoral

Se elige el Presidente de los Estados Unidos indirectamente a través de los "electores," quienes componen el Colegio Electoral, más bien que directamente por la gente, o por voto popular. Este método indirecto requiere que un candidato reciba 270 votos electorales para ganar la Presidencia. Nuestro Colegio Electoral es una herencia magnífica, pasado a nosotros por los Fundadores de la nación. Ha servido los Estados Unidos de América por más de 200 años y fue probado, como nunca antes, durante las elecciones presidenciales del año 2000.

Sugerencias sobre la votación

- Usted no tiene que votar por todo lo que sale en la balota. Puede votar apenas por la persona o el asunto en lo cual le interese.

- No tire su balota de muestra. Ésta le dice adonde ir a votar, que se llama su "centro electoral." Le da también la oportunidad de poner en práctica el votar.

- Si usted desea un voto por correo, utilice la solicitud que aparece con su balota de muestra.

- Lleve la balota de práctica con usted cuando va a votar. Esto hace la votación más fácil y más pronto, también.

Conocer a nuestro América

Hacer cosas tal como el guardar las fiestas tradicionales nacionales, recitar la Promesa de Fidelidad en la escuela y cantar el himno nacional con otros espectadores en alguna festividad son maneras en las cuales usted puede hacerse parte de las costumbres americanas. Repase las páginas que siguen y familiarícese con algunas canciones, símbolos y días festivos de su nuevo país.

What can you *do* for your country after naturalization? *Become informed and then vote!* Becoming informed is made easy today by television, radio, newspapers, magazines and even the internet.

Well-informed citizens know what is going on in their community, in their nation, and around the world. They learn about the candidates who are running for office. They base their opinion on facts and then decide who they think is the best-qualified candidate and what is best for their community, state, and country. Thomas Jefferson, our country's third President, recognized this when he wrote:

> ". . . whenever things get so far wrong as to attract their notice, the people, if well informed, may be relied on to set them to rights."

How better than voting to set wrongs "to rights?" Additionally, of course, you can express your opinion by writing your Congressman or the editor of a local newspaper.

Registering to vote

In order to vote, you must first register. As there are time requirements (sometimes about 29 days before an election), it is a good idea to be prepared by registering to vote as soon as you become a citizen. Do this in the community where you live. If you move, you must register again in your new community. To register, you must:

- Be a citizen of the United States.

- Be a resident of the state or community where you vote.

- Be at least 18 years old by election day (per Amendment 26 of the Constitution).

- Not be in prison or on parole for a felony conviction.

Registering is very simple and takes only a few minutes. Just fill out a voter registration card similarly to the sample on page 113.

El Credo Americano
por William Tyler Page

Yo creo en los Estados Unidos de América como un Gobierno de la gente, por la gente y para la gente; cuyos poderes justos se derivan del consentimiento de los gobernados; una democracia en una República; una Nación soberana de muchos estados soberanos; una Unión perfecta, una e inseparable; estable-cida sobre los principios de libertad, igualdad, justicia y humanidad por cual los patriotas americanos sacrificaron sus vidas y sus fortunas.

Por eso, creo que es mi deber a mi país apoyar su Constitución, obedecer sus leyes, respetar su bandera, y defenderlo contra todos enemigos.

El Credo Americano fue el resultado de una competencia a escala nacional para escribir un Credo Nacional, lo cual sería un resumen abreviado de la fe política americana fundado sobre las tradiciones fundamentales y la historia americana. Más de 3,000 entradas fueron recibidas y entre ellas le declararon la de William Tyler Page el ganador. El gobierno de los EE. UU. adoptó el Credo en 1918.

Nuestro Himno Nacional
"La Bandera Centelleada de Estrellas"
por Francis Scott Key

¡Oiga! ¿No puedes ver, a la luz del amenecer,

Lo que orgullosamente alabamos en el ocaso del crepúsculo?

Cuyos anchas franjas y estrellas brillantes, en batalla peligrosa,

Desde los bastiones las vimos galanas ondeando.

Y los cohetes refulgentes y las bombas estallando en el aire,

Dieron prueba durante la noche que nuestra bandera ahí estaba.

¡Oiga! ¿Ondea todavía la bandera centelleada de estrellas

Sobre la tierra de la gente libre y el hogar de los valientes?

Francis Scott Key, fue inspirado a escribir las palabras de "La Bandera Centelleada de Estrellas, " cuando vió la bandera todavía ondeándose sobre la Fuerte McHenry, después de un ataque británico en 1814. El Presidente Woodrow Wilson mandó a los servicios militares tocar el himno en 1916. Fue designado el Himno Nacional por el Congreso en 1931. Típicamente, los americanos cantan el himno antes de los juegos deportivos como el fútbol americano o el béisbol. En realidad, el Himno Nacional consiste en cuatro stanzas, de las cuales se conoce más el primer verso.

Sample 7: Voter Registration Card

A Voter Registration card may be obtained in person from such places as libraries, post offices, city halls, and the Department of Motor Vehicles. Then, just mail it in. Or, you may visit the Registrar of Voters office to register in person. The phone number for the Registrar of Voters in your community may be obtained either from Directory Assistance or from the front of the telephone book under "government" listings.

The card may differ slightly from community to community, but basically they all require the same information. Notice that you are to check your "political party" affiliation, the one you believe in. If you don't know or don't want anyone else to know, be sure to check "Decline to state." It is your privilege to do so. Just don't leave any blanks. Check something! Otherwise, your card may be considered incomplete, and you won't be registered.

Popular vs. electoral voting

The President of the United Sates is elected indirectly through electors, who make up the Electoral College, rather than directly by the people, or by popular vote. This indirect method requires a candidate to receive 270 electoral votes to win the

Nuestro Lema Nacional, "In God We Trust" (En Dios Confiamos)

El Lema Nacional, "In God We Trust" (En Dios Confiamos) apareció primero en las monedas de los EE. UU. en 1864. Fue agregado para reconocer al Dios todopoderoso en la moneda de nuestra nación. En los años desde 1864, el lema ha desaparecido y reaparecido en varias monedas hasta 1955. Ése era cuando el Congreso mandó colocarlo en toda la moneda corriente de los EE.UU. Se ha desafiado el uso del lema en los tribunales muchas veces durante los años que ha estado en uso. No obstante, en cada vez se ha sido sostenido en nuestros tribunales nacionales.

Nuestro Ave Nacional, el águila calvo

El águila calvo, el más conocido entre los águilas norteamericanos, se representa en el Gran Sello de los Estados Unidos. En realidad no es calvo; fue nombrado así por su cabeza blanca. Los águilas simbolizan la potencia, el valor y la libertad. El Congreso adoptó un diseño visualizado del águila calvo para el Gran Sello de los Estados Unidos, y el águila calvo se convirtió en el Ave Nacional.

Presidency. Our Electoral College is a grand legacy given to us by our nation's founding fathers. It has served the United States of America for more than 200 years and was tested, like never before, during the 2000 Presidential election.

Hints about voting

- You don't have to vote for everything on the ballot. You can vote just for the person or issue that you know about or that interests you.

- Don't throw away your sample ballot. It tells where to go to vote, which is called your "polling place." It also gives you an opportunity to practice voting.

- If you want an absentee ballot, use the application appearing with your sample ballot.

- Take your practice ballot with you to the polls. This makes voting much easier and quicker, too.

Knowing our America

Doing things such as observing traditional national holidays, reciting the Pledge of Allegiance at school, and singing the national anthem along with the crowd at events are some of the ways that help you to become a part of the American way of life. Browse through the following pages in the book to familiarize yourself with some of the songs, symbols and holidays of your new country.

The American's Creed
by William Tyler Page

I believe in the United States of America as a government of the people, by the people, for the people; whose just powers are derived from the consent of the governed, a democracy in a republic, a sovereign Nation of many sovereign States; a perfect union, one and inseparable; established upon those principles of freedom, equality, justice, and humanity for which American patriots sacrificed their lives and fortunes.

I therefore believe it is my duty to my country to love it, to support its Constitution, to obey its laws, to respect its flag, and to defend it against all enemies.

The American's Creed was the result of a nationwide contest to write a National Creed, which would be a brief summary of the American political faith founded upon things fundamental in American history and tradition. Over 3,000 entries were received and William Tyler Page's was declared the winner. The U.S. government adopted the Creed in 1918.

El Gran Sello de los Estados Unidos

El 4 de julio, 1776, el Congreso Continental designó un comité que consistía en Benjamin Franklin, John Adams and Thomas Jefferson, para "traer un estratagema para un sello de los Estados Unidos de América." Las sumisiones, los rechazamientos, y las demoras que sucedieron fueron numerosos. Finalmente en 1782, el Congreso aprobó este diseño de un águila con alas extendidas, blandiendo las flechas de guerra y la rama del olivo de la paz. Simbólicamente, el sello refleja las creencias y los valores que los fundadores deseaban atribuir a la nueva nación y de lo que deseaban pasar a sus descendientes. Se limita estrictamente por ley el uso del sello y no puede ser utilizado para los propósitos comerciales para indicar un endoso del gobierno de un producto o servicio.

La Estatua de Libertad

La Estatua de Libertad era un regalo de la amistad internacional de la gente de Francia a la gente de los Estados Unidos. Está situada en la Isla de Ellis, en el puerto de Nueva York, fue dedicada en 1886, y designada como Monumento Nacional en 1924. La antorcha de libertad presagia una recepción a todos, igual que el "Coloso Nuevo," que lee en parte:

> *"¡Déme sus cansados, sus pobres,*
>
> *Sus masas amontonadas, anhelando respirar libremente,*
>
> *Los miserables de sus orillas abundantes.*
>
> *Envíeme estos, el nomada, sacudidos por la tempestad,*
>
> *Me levanto mi lámpara al lado de la puerta dorada!"*

Los siete rayos de la corona de la estatua representan los siete mares y continentes del mundo. La tabilla, la cual la estatua sostiene en la mano izquierda lee (en números romanos) "4 de julio, 1776," y la altura desde el nivel del suelo hasta la punta de arriba de la antorchamide 305

Our National Anthem, "The Star-Spangled Banner"
by Francis Scott Key

Oh, say, can you see, by the dawn's early light,

> *What so proudly we hailed at the twilight's last gleaming?*

Whose broad stripes and bright stars, thro' the perilous fight

> *O'er the ramparts we watched, were so gallantly streaming.*

And the rockets red glare, the bombs bursting in air,

> *Gave proof through the night that our flag was still there.*

Oh, say, does that star-spangled banner yet wave

> *O'er the land of the free and the home of the brave?*

Francis Scott Key, inspired by seeing the American flag still flying after an 1814 British attack on Fort McHenry, wrote the words to "The Star-Spangled Banner." President Woodrow Wilson ordered the military services to play the anthem in 1916. It was designated the National Anthem by Congress in 1931. Americans typically sing the anthem before sporting events such as football and baseball. The National Anthem actually consists of four stanzas, with the first verse above being the most well-known.

Our National Motto, "In God We Trust"

The National Motto "In God We Trust" first appeared on some U.S. coins in 1864. It was added as means to recognize the almighty God on our nation's coins. In the years since 1864, the motto has disappeared and reappeared on various coins until 1955. That is when Congress ordered it placed on *all* U.S. currency. The use of the motto has been challenged in court many times over the years it has been in use. However, it has been upheld each and every time in our nation's courts.

pies. Después de dos años de restauración, había un espectáculo de cuatro días de conciertos, buques antiguos, festivales étnicas y fuegos artificiales desde el 3 a 6 de julio, 1986, celebrando el aniversario 100.

Días festivos

Estos son los días festivos que generalmente celebran los americanos. ¡Tome parte en las festividades!

Año Nuevo .... 1 de enero

Día de Martin Luther King, Jr. .... tercer lunes de enero

El Día del Presidentes .... tercer lunes de febrero

Viernes Santo .... el viernes antes de la Pascua

El Día del Recuerdo .... último lunes de mayo

Día de la Independencia .... 4 de julio

Día de Trabajo .... primer lunes de septiembre

Día de Colón......................... segundo lunes de octubre

Día del Veteranos.................... segundo lunes de noviembre

Día de Gracias .... cuarto jueves de noviembre

Navidad .... 25 de diciembre

En los días festivos, el cierre de las oficinas del gobierno, los negocios y las escuelas varía. Si un día festivo cae en domingo o sábado, se le observe usualmente el siguiente lunes o el viernes anterior.

Our National Bird, the bald eagle

The bald eagle, the best known of the North American eagles, is depicted on the Great Seal of the United States. It is not really bald; it was named for its white head. Eagles symbolize power, courage and freedom. Congress adopted a design displaying the bald eagle for the Great Seal of the United States, and the bald eagle became our National Bird.

The Great Seal of the United States

On July 4, 1776, the Continental Congress appointed a committee consisting of Benjamin Franklin, John Adams and Thomas Jefferson, "to bring in a device for a seal of the United States of America." Numerous committee submissions, rejections and delays occurred. In 1782 the Congress finally approved this design, a spread-winged bald eagle brandishing the arrows of war and the olive branch of peace. Symbolically the seal reflects the beliefs and values that the founding fathers attached to the new nation and wished to pass on to their decedents. Use of this seal is strictly limited by law and cannot be used for commercial purposes to denote a government endorsement of a product or service.

The Statue of Liberty

The Statue of Liberty was a gift of international friendship from the people of France to the people of the United States. It is located on Ellis Island in New York

Harbor, was dedicated in 1886, and designated as a National Monument in 1924. The liberty torch bids a welcome to all, as does the "New Colossus," which reads in part:

"Give me your tired, your poor,

Your huddled masses yearning to breathe free,

The wretched refuse of your teeming shore.

Send these, the homeless, tempest-tossed
   to me,

I lift my lamp beside the golden door!"

The seven rays of the statue's crown represent the seven seas and continents of the world. The tablet, which the statue holds in her left hand, reads (in roman numerals) "July 4, 1776," and the height from ground level to the tip of the torch measures 305 feet. After two years of restoration, there was a four-day extravaganza of concerts, tall ships, ethnic festivals, and fireworks from July 3 to 6, 1986, celebrating the 100th anniversary.

Holidays

These are among the holidays most widely celebrated by Americans. Join in and become part of the festivities!

New Year's Day .... January 1

Martin Luther King, Jr. Day .... 3rd Monday in January

Presidents' Day .... 3rd Monday in February

Good Friday .... Friday before Easter

Memorial Day .... Last Monday in May

Independence Day .... July 4

Labor Day .... 1st Monday in September

Columbus Day .... 2nd Monday in October

Veterans Day .... 2nd Monday in November

Thanksgiving Day .... 4th Thursday in November

Christmas .... December 25

Government, business and school closing practices vary for the holidays. If the holiday happens to fall on a Sunday or a Saturday, it is usually observed on the following Monday or the Friday before.

Apéndice Uno
Circunstancias Especiales Calificativas

Algunos solicitantes tienen circunstancias especiales, que sirven como base para solictar la naturalización. Un base quiere decir una circunstancia calificativa que cumple con el requisito de *"tipo de solicitante."* Aquí están las circunstancias especiales que califican:

1. Servido en una nave operado por los Estados Unidos.

2. Servido en una nave registrada en los Estados Unidos.

3. Un empleado o persona bajo contrato del gobierno estadounidense.

4. Una persona que desempeña funciones ministerios o sacerdotal para una denominación religiosa o para una organización interdenominacional con una presencia válida en los Estados Unidos.*

5. Empleado por uno de los siguientes:*

   a. Una institución americana de investigación.

   b. Una corporación o negocio de propiedad americana que se desempeña en el desarrollo de comercio y negocio extranjero.

   c. Una organización internacional pública de la cual es miembro por ley o tratado de los Estados Unidos.

6. Haber estado empleado por 5 años o más por una organización no lucrativa que propone los intereses de los Estados Unidos al extranjero por los medios de comunicaciones.

7. Ser esposo(a) de un ciudadano de los EE.UU. quien es (a o b, *y* c):

   a. Un miembro de las Fuerzas Armadas de los EE.UU.

   b. Tener una circunstancia calificativa del párrafo 3 a 5.

   c. *Y,* su esposo(a) ciudadano debe de estar trabajando en el extranjero por al menos 1 año según el contrato del empleo.

Esta lista describe brevamente las circunstancias especiales reconocidas por el INS. Comuníquese con el INS o un abogado de inmigración para más información detallada, si piensa que usted califique bajo algunas de estas circunstancias especiales.

---

* Acto de Inmigración y Nacionalidad (Sección 319)

Appendix One
Qualifying Special Circumstances

A few applicants may have special circumstances, which can be used as a basis for applying for naturalization. A basis means a qualifying circumstance to satisfy the *"type of applicant"* requirement. Here are the qualifying special circumstances:

1. Served on a vessel operated by the United States.

2. Served on a vessel registered in the United States.

3. An employee or person under contract to the U.S. Government.

4. A person who performs ministerial or priestly functions for a religious denomination or an interdenominational organization with a valid presence in the United States.*

5. Employed by one of the following:*

   a. An American institution of research;

   b. An American-owned firm or corporation engaged in developing foreign trade and commerce for U.S;

   c. A public international organization of which the United States is a member by law or treaty.

6. Have been employed for 5 years or more by a U.S. nonprofit organization that promotes the interest of the U.S. abroad through the communication media.

7. Are a spouse of a U.S. citizen who is (a or b, *and* c):

   a. A member of the U.S. Armed Forces;

   b. Has any qualifying circumstance from paragraph 3 thru 5.

   c. *And*, your citizen spouse must be working overseas for at least 1 year according to an employment contract.

This list briefly describes the special circumstances recognized by the INS. Contact either the INS or an immigration attorney for more detailed information if you think you may qualify under a special circumstance.

---

*Immigration and Nationality Act (Section 319)

Apéndice Dos
Formulario FD-258 — La Tarjeta de Huellas Dactilares

¡Importante! Solamente los *solicitantes de ultramar* entregan la tarjeta de huellas dactilares *con* un N-400. Todos los demás deben esperar para una cita de las huellas dactilares, la cual el INS le enviará a usted, *después* de que usted ha entregado su solicitud N-400.

Appendix Two
Form FD-258 — Fingerprint Card

APPLICANT	LEAVE BLANK	TYPE OR PRINT ALL INFORMATION IN BLACK		FBI	LEAVE BLANK

LAST NAME <u>NAM</u>   FIRST NAME   MIDDLE NAME

SIGNATURE OF PERSON FINGERPRINTED

ALIASES <u>AKA</u>

ORI

CAINSSF00
USINS
SAN FRANCISCO, CA

RESIDENCE OF PERSON FINGERPRINTED

DATE OF BIRTH <u>DOB</u>
Month Day Year

CITIZENSHIP <u>CTZ</u>

SEX	RACE	HGT.	WGT.	EYES	HAIR	PLACE OF BIRTH <u>POB</u>

DATE SIGNATURE OF OFFICIAL TAKING FINGERPRINTS

YOUR NO. <u>OCA</u>

LEAVE BLANK

EMPLOYER AND ADDRESS

FBI NO. <u>FBI</u>

CLASS _____

ARMED FORCES NO. <u>MNU</u>

REASON FINGERPRINTED

SOCIAL SECURITY NO. <u>SOC</u>

REF. _____

MISCELLANEOUS NO. <u>MNU</u>

1. R. THUMB	2. R. INDEX	3. R. MIDDLE	4. R. RING	5. R. LITTLE

6. L. THUMB	7. L. INDEX	8. L. MIDDLE	9. L. RING	10. L. LITTLE

LEFT FOUR FINGERS TAKEN SIMULTANEOUSLY	L. THUMB	R. THUMB	RIGHT FOUR FINGERS TAKEN SIMUTANEOUSLY

Important! A completed fingerprint card is only submitted *with* an N-400 by *overseas filers*. All others must wait for a fingerprinting appointment, which will be mailed to you by the INS, *after* filing your N-400 application.

Apéndice Tres
Trece Agencias Nacionales para el Pasaporte

Boston Passport Agency
Thomas P. O'Neill Federal Building
10 Causeway Street, Suite 247
Boston, MA 02222-1094
617-878-0900

Chicago Passport Agency
Kluczynski Federal Office Building
230 South Dearborn Street, 18th Floor
Chicago, IL 60604-1564
312-341-6020

Connecticut Passport Agency
50 Washington Street
Norwalk, CT 06854
203-299-5443

Honolulu Passport Agency
Prince Kuhio Federal Building
300 Ala Moana Boulevard, Suite 1-330
Honolulu, HI 96850
808-522-8283

Houston Passport Agency
Mickey Leland Federal Building
1919 Smith Street, Suite 1400
Houston, TX 77002-8049
713-751-0294

Los Angeles Passport Agency
11000 Wilshire Boulevard, Suite 1000
Los Angeles, CA 90024-3615
310-575-5700

Miami Passport Agency
Claude Pepper Federal Office Building
51 SW First Avenue, 3rd Floor
Miami, FL 33130-1680
305-539-3600

New Orleans Passport Agency
One Canal Place
365 Canal Street, Suite 1300
New Orleans, LA 70130-6508
504 412-2600

New York Passport Agency
376 Hudson Street
New York, NY 10014
212-206-3500

Philadelphia Passport Agency
U.S. Custom House
200 Chestnut Street, Room 103
Philadelphia, PA 19106-2970
215-418-5937

San Francisco Passport Agency
95 Hawthorne Street, 5th Floor
San Francisco, CA 94105-3901
415-538-2700

Seattle Passport Agency
Henry Jackson Federal Building
915 Second Avenue, Suite 992
Seattle, WA 98174-1091
206-808-5700

Washington Passport Agency
1111 19th Street, N.W.
Washington, DC 20524
202-647-0518

Appendix Three
Thirteen Nationwide Passport Agencies

Boston Passport Agency
Thomas P. O'Neill Federal Building
10 Causeway Street, Suite 247
Boston, MA 02222-1094
617-878-0900

Chicago Passport Agency
Kluczynski Federal Office Building
230 South Dearborn Street, 18th Floor
Chicago, IL 60604-1564
312-341-6020

Connecticut Passport Agency
50 Washington Street
Norwalk, CT 06854
203-299-5443

Honolulu Passport Agency
Prince Kuhio Federal Building
300 Ala Moana Boulevard, Suite 1-330
Honolulu, HI 96850
808-522-8283

Houston Passport Agency
Mickey Leland Federal Building
1919 Smith Street, Suite 1400
Houston, TX 77002-8049
713-751-0294

Los Angeles Passport Agency
11000 Wilshire Boulevard, Suite 1000
Los Angeles, CA 90024-3615
310-575-5700

Miami Passport Agency
Claude Pepper Federal Office Building
51 SW First Avenue, 3rd Floor
Miami, FL 33130-1680
305-539-3600

New Orleans Passport Agency
One Canal Place
365 Canal Street, Suite 1300
New Orleans, LA 70130-6508
504 412-2600

New York Passport Agency
376 Hudson Street
New York, NY 10014
212-206-3500

Philadelphia Passport Agency
U.S. Custom House
200 Chestnut Street, Room 103
Philadelphia, PA 19106-2970
215-418-5937

San Francisco Passport Agency
95 Hawthorne Street, 5th Floor
San Francisco, CA 94105-3901
415-538-2700

Seattle Passport Agency
Henry Jackson Federal Building
915 Second Avenue, Suite 992
Seattle, WA 98174-1091
206-808-5700

Washington Passport Agency
1111 19th Street, N.W.
Washington, DC 20524
202-647-0518

Appendix Four

Constitution

of the United States of America

The oldest living constitution in the world!

Preamble

We the People of the United States,

More perfect than original existing league of states

in Order to form a more perfect Union,

establish Justice, insure domestic Tranquility,

provide for the common defence,

promote the general Welfare,

and secure the Blessings of Liberty

to ourselves and our Posterity,

do ordain and establish this Constitution

for the United States of America.

A government of *people*

Article 1: Legislative branch

Article I

Section 1. All legislative Powers herein granted shall be vested in a Congress of the United States, which shall consist of a Senate and House of Representatives.

Sets up a two-house system: Senate and House of Representatives

About the House of Representatives

Section 2. The House of Representatives shall be composed of Members chosen every second Year by the People of the several States, and the Electors in each State shall have the Qualifications requisite for Electors of the most numerous Branch of the State Legislature.

No Person shall be a Representative who shall not have attained to the Age of twenty five Years, and been seven Years a Citizen of the United States, and who shall not, when elected, be an Inhabitant of that State in which he shall be chosen.

Representatives and direct Taxes shall be apportioned among the several States which may be included within this Union, according to their respective Numbers, which shall be determined by adding to the whole Number of free Persons, including those bound to Service for a Term of Years, and excluding Indians not taxed, three fifths of all other Persons. The actual Enumeration shall be made within three Years after the first Meeting of the Congress of the United States, and within every subsequent Term of ten Years, in such Manner as they shall by Law direct. The Number of Representatives shall not exceed one for every thirty Thousand, but each State shall have at Least one Representative; and until such enumeration shall be made, the State of New Hampshire shall be entitled to choose three, Massachusetts eight, Rhode-Island and Providence Plantations one, Connecticut five, New-York six, New Jersey four, Pennsylvania eight, Delaware one, Maryland six, Virginia ten, North Carolina five, South Carolina five, and Georgia three.

When vacancies happen in the Representation from any State, the Executive Authority thereof shall issue Writs of Election to fill such Vacancies.

The House of Representatives shall choose their Speaker and other Officers; and shall have the sole Power of Impeachment.

Section 3. The Senate of the United States shall be composed of two Senators from each State, chosen by the Legislature thereof, for six Years; and each Senator shall have one Vote.

Immediately after they shall be assembled in Consequence of the first Election, they shall be divided as equally as may be into three Classes. The Seats of the Senators of the first Class shall be vacated at the Expiration of the second Year, of the second Class at the Expiration of the fourth Year, and of the third Class at the Expiration of the sixth Year, so

---

See *income tax* Amendment 16

Congress takes a *census* every 10 years

Year	Population
1790	3,929,214
2000	281,424,177

Impeachment means *accusation*

Changed by Amendment 17 (to a direct vote by the people)

435 Representatives

About the Senate

100 Senators

that one third may be chosen every second Year; and if Vacancies happen by Resignation, or otherwise, during the Recess of the Legislature of any State, the Executive thereof may make temporary Appointments until the next Meeting of the Legislature, which shall then fill such Vacancies.

No Person shall be a Senator who shall not have attained to the Age of thirty Years, and been nine Years a Citizen of the United States, and who shall not, when elected, be an Inhabitant of that State for which he shall be chosen.

The Vice President casts the deciding vote in case of a tie

The Vice President of the United States shall be President of the Senate, but shall have no Vote, unless they be equally divided.

The Senate shall choose their other Officers, and also a President pro tempore, in the Absence of the Vice President, or when he shall exercise the Office of President of the United States.

The Senate shall have the sole Power to try all Impeachments. When sitting for that Purpose, they shall be on Oath or Affirmation. When the President of the United States is tried, the Chief Justice shall preside: And no Person shall be convicted without the Concurrence of two thirds of the Members present.

Puts *limits* on punishment

Judgment in Cases of Impeachment shall not extend further than to removal from Office, and disqualification to hold and enjoy any Office of honor, Trust or Profit under the United States: but the Party convicted shall nevertheless be liable and subject to Indictment, Trial, Judgment and Punishment, according to Law.

About *elections* and *meetings*

Section 4. The Times, Places and Manner of holding Elections for Senators and Representatives, shall be prescribed in each State by the Legislature thereof; but the Congress may at any time by Law make or alter such Regulations, except as to the Places of choosing Senators.

The Congress shall assemble at least once in every Year, and such Meeting shall be on the first Monday in December, unless they shall by Law appoint a different Day.

Changed by Amendment 20

Section 5. Each House shall be the Judge of the Elections, Returns and Qualifications of its own Members, and a Majority of each shall constitute a Quorum to do Business; but a smaller Number may adjourn from day to day, and may be authorized to compel the Attendance of absent Members, in such Manner, and under such Penalties as each House may provide.

About rules of order

Each House may determine the Rules of its Proceedings, punish its Members for disorderly Behavior, and, with the Concurrence of two thirds, expel a Member.

Each House shall keep a Journal of its Proceedings, and from time to time publish the same, excepting such Parts as may in their Judgment require Secrecy; and the Yeas and Nays of the Members of either House on any question shall, at the Desire of one fifth of those Present, be entered on the Journal.

Neither House, during the Session of Congress, shall, without the Consent of the other, adjourn for more than three days, nor to any other Place than that in which the two Houses shall be sitting.

Neither House can go *on strike!*

Section 6. The Senators and Representatives shall receive a Compensation for their Services, to be ascertained by Law, and paid out of the Treasury of the United States. They shall in all Cases, except Treason, Felony and Breach of the Peace, be privileged from Arrest during their Attendance at the Session of their respective Houses, and in going to and returning from the same; and for any Speech or Debate in either House, they shall not be questioned in any other Place.

About pay and privileges

An *American* idea—to *pay* legislators!

No Senator or Representative shall, during the Time for which he was elected, be appointed to any civil Office under the Authority of the United States, which shall have been created, or the Emoluments whereof shall have been increased during such time; and no Person holding any Office under the United States, shall be a Member of either House during his Continuance in Office.

About how Bills become Laws

Section 7. All Bills for raising Revenue shall originate in the House of Representatives; but the Senate may propose or concur with Amendments as on other Bills.

Checks and balances

Pocket veto

Every Bill which shall have passed the House of Representatives and the Senate, shall, before it become a Law, be presented to the President of the United States; If he approve he shall sign it, but if not he shall return it, with his Objections to that House in which it shall have originated, who shall enter the Objections at large on their Journal, and proceed to reconsider it. If after such Reconsideration two thirds of that House shall agree to pass the Bill, it shall be sent, together with the Objections, to the other House, by which it shall likewise be reconsidered, and if approved by two thirds of that House, it shall become a Law. But in all such Cases the Votes of both Houses shall be determined by yeas and Nays, and the Names of the Persons voting for and against the Bill shall be entered on the Journal of each House respectively. If any Bill shall not be returned by the President within ten Days (Sundays excepted) after it shall have been presented to him, the Same shall be a Law, in like Manner as if he had signed it, unless the Congress by their Adjournment prevent its Return, in which Case it shall not be a Law.

Every Order, Resolution, or Vote to which the Concurrence of the Senate and House of Representatives may be necessary (except on a question of Adjournment) shall be presented to the President of the United States; and before the Same shall take Effect, shall be approved by him, or being disapproved by him, shall be re-passed by two thirds of the Senate and House of Representatives, according to the Rules and Limitations prescribed in the Case of a Bill.

About the *powers of Congress*

Section 8. The Congress shall have Power To lay and collect Taxes, Duties, Imposts and Excises, to pay the Debts and provide for the common Defense and general Welfare of the United States; but all Duties, Imposts and Excises shall be uniform throughout the United States;

Taxation

To borrow Money on the credit of the United States;

Borrow money

To regulate Commerce with foreign Nations, and among the several States, and with the Indian Tribes;

Foreign trade

To establish an uniform Rule of Naturalization, and uniform Laws on the subject of Bankruptcies throughout the United States;

Naturalization

Bankruptcy

To coin Money, regulate the Value thereof, and of foreign Coin, and fix the Standard of Weights and Measures;

Money

To provide for the Punishment of counterfeiting the Securities and current Coin of the United States;

Counterfeiting

To establish Post Offices and post Roads;

Post offices

Copyrights and patents

To promote the Progress of Science and useful Arts, by securing for limited Times to Authors and Inventors the exclusive Right to their respective Writings and Discoveries;

To constitute Tribunals inferior to the supreme Court;

Federal courts

To define and punish Piracies and Felonies committed on the high Seas, and Offences against the Law of Nations;

Maritime crimes

To declare War, grant Letters of Marque and Reprisal, and make Rules concerning Captures on Land and Water;

War

Armed forces

To raise and support Armies, but no Appropriation of Money to that Use shall be for a longer Term than two Years;

To provide and maintain a Navy;

To make Rules for the Government and Regulation of the land and naval Forces;

Militia

To provide for calling forth the Militia to execute the Laws of the Union, suppress Insurrections and repel Invasions;

To provide for organizing, arming, and disciplining, the Militia, and for governing such Part of them as may be employed in the Service of the United States, reserving to the States respectively, the Appointment of the Officers, and the Authority of training the Militia according to the discipline prescribed by Congress;

District of Columbia

To exercise exclusive Legislation in all Cases whatsoever, over such District (not exceeding ten Miles square) as may, by Cession of particular States, and the Acceptance of Congress, become the Seat of the Government of the United States, and to exercise like Authority over all Places purchased by the Consent of the Legislature of the State in which the Same shall be, for the Erection of Forts, Magazines, Arsenals, dock-Yards, and other needful Buildings; And

Make laws

To make all Laws which shall be necessary and proper for carrying into Execution the foregoing Powers, and all other Powers vested by this Constitution in the Government of the United States, or in any Department or Officer thereof.

About powers *forbidden* to *Congress*

Section 9. The Migration or Importation of such Persons as any of the States now existing shall think proper to admit, shall not be prohibited by the Congress prior to the Year one thousand eight hundred and eight, but a Tax or duty may be imposed on such Importation, not exceeding ten dollars for each Person.

The Privilege of the Writ of Habeas Corpus shall not be suspended, unless when in Cases of Rebellion or Invasion the public Safety may require it.

No Bill of Attainder or ex post facto Law shall be passed.

No Capitation, or other direct, Tax shall be laid, unless in Proportion to the Census or Enumeration herein before directed to be taken.

No Tax or Duty shall be laid on Articles exported from any State.

No Preference shall be given by any Regulation of Commerce or Revenue to the Ports of one State over those of another: nor shall Vessels bound to, or from, one State, be obliged to enter, clear, or pay Duties in another.

No Money shall be drawn from the Treasury, but in Consequence of Appropriations made by Law; and a regular Statement and Account of the Receipts and Expenditures of all public Money shall be published from time to time.

No Title of Nobility shall be granted by the United States: And no Person holding any Office of Profit or Trust under them, shall, without the Consent of the Congress, accept of any present, Emolument, Office, or Title, of any kind whatever, from any King, Prince, or foreign State.

Section 10. No State shall enter into any Treaty, Alliance, or Confederation; grant Letters of Marque and Reprisal; coin Money; emit Bills of Credit; make any Thing but gold and silver Coin a Tender in Payment of Debts; pass any Bill of Attainder, ex post facto Law, or Law impairing the Obligation of Contracts, or grant any Title of Nobility.

No State shall, without the Consent of the Congress, lay any Imposts or Duties on Imports or Exports, except what may be absolutely necessary for executing it's inspection Laws: and the net Produce

Ex post facto: a law that makes criminal an act that was legal when committed

About powers *forbidden* to *states*

Habeas corpus: a court order designed to prevent illegal arrests and unlawful imprisonment

No title of nobility (King, Queen, Prince, Princess, etc.)

No treaties, coining money, titles of nobility, etc.

No duties on imports or exports

of all Duties and Imposts, laid by any State on Imports or Exports, shall be for the Use of the Treasury of the United States; and all such Laws shall be subject to the Revision and Control of the Congress.

No foreign agreements or war powers

No State shall, without the Consent of Congress, lay any Duty of Tonnage, keep Troops, or Ships of War in time of Peace, enter into any Agreement or Compact with another State, or with a foreign Power, or engage in War, unless actually invaded, or in such imminent Danger as will not admit of delay.

Article 2: Executive branch

Article II

Section 1. The executive Power shall be vested in a President of the United States of America. He shall hold his Office during the Term of four Years, and, together with the Vice President, chosen for the same Term, be elected, as follows:

Each State shall appoint, in such Manner as the Legislature thereof may direct, a Number of Electors, equal to the whole Number of Senators and Representatives to which the State may be entitled in the Congress: but no Senator or Representative, or Person holding an Office of Trust or Profit under the United States, shall be appointed an Elector.

The Electors shall meet in their respective States, and vote by Ballot for two Persons, of whom one at least shall not be an Inhabitant of the same State with themselves. And they shall make a List of all the Persons voted for, and of the Number of Votes for each; which List they shall sign and certify, and transmit sealed to the Seat of the Government of the United States, directed to the President of the Senate. The President of the Senate shall, in the Presence of the Senate and House of Representatives, open all the Certificates, and the Votes shall then be counted. The Person having the greatest Number of Votes shall be the President, if such Number be a Majority of the whole Number of Electors appointed; and if there be

Amendment 12 supersedes this

more than one who have such Majority, and have an equal Number of Votes, then the House of Representatives shall immediately choose by Ballot one of them for President; and if no Person have a Majority, then from the five highest on the List the said House shall in like Manner choose the President. But in choosing the President, the Votes shall be taken by States, the Representation from each State having one Vote; A quorum for this Purpose shall consist of a Member or Members from two thirds of the States, and a Majority of all the States shall be necessary to a Choice. In every Case, after the Choice of the President, the Person having the greatest Number of Votes of the Electors shall be the Vice President. But if there should remain two or more who have equal Votes, the Senate shall choose from them by Ballot the Vice President.

First *Tuesday* after first Monday in *November*

The Congress may determine the Time of choosing the Electors, and the Day on which they shall give their Votes; which Day shall be the same throughout the United States.

No Person except a natural born Citizen, or a Citizen of the United States, at the time of the Adoption of this Constitution, shall be eligible to the Office of President; neither shall any Person be eligible to that Office who shall not have attained to the Age of thirty five Years, and been fourteen Years a Resident within the United States.

Qualifications for *President*:
- Natural born citizen
- Age 35 minimum
- 14 years a U.S. resident (minimum)

Sets forth succession

In Case of the Removal of the President from Office, or of his Death, Resignation, or Inability to discharge the Powers and Duties of the said Office the Same shall devolve on the Vice President, and the Congress may by Law provide for the Case of Removal, Death, Resignation or Inability, both of the President and Vice President, declaring what Officer shall then act as President, and such Officer shall act accordingly, until the Disability be removed, or a President shall be elected.

See also Amendment 25

Provides for a salary for the President The President shall, at stated Times, receive for his Services, a Compensation, which shall neither be increased nor diminished during the Period for which he shall have been elected, and he shall not receive within that Period any other Emolument from the United States, or any of them.

Before he enter on the Execution of his Office, he shall take the following Oath or Affirmation:—

Oath of Office "I do solemnly swear (or affirm) that I will faithfully execute the Office of President of the United States, and will to the best of my Ability, preserve, protect and defend the Constitution of the United States."

About Presidential powers **Section 2.** The President shall be Commander in Chief of the Army and Navy of the United States, and of the Militia of the several States, when called into the actual Service of the United States; he may require the Opinion, in writing, of the principal Officer in each of the executive Departments, upon any Subject relating to the Duties of their respective Offices, and he shall have Power to grant Reprieves and Pardons for Offences against the United States, except in Cases of Impeachment.

Only Congress can declare war

Origin of *cabinet* idea

He shall have Power, by and with the Advice and Consent of the Senate, to make Treaties, provided two thirds of the Senators present concur; and he shall nominate, and by and with the Advice and Consent of the Senate, shall appoint Ambassadors, other public Ministers and Consuls, Judges of the supreme Court, and all other Officers of the United States, whose Appointments are not herein otherwise provided for, and which shall be established by Law: but the Congress may by Law vest the Appointment of such inferior Officers, as they think proper, in the President alone, in the Courts of Law, or in the Heads of Departments.

The President shall have Power to fill up all Vacancies that may happen during the Recess of the

Senate, by granting Commissions which shall expire at the End of their next Session.

About Presidential duties

Section 3. He shall from time to time give to the Congress Information of the State of the Union, and recommend to their Consideration such Measures as he shall judge necessary and expedient; he may, on extraordinary Occasions, convene both Houses, or either of them, and in Case of Disagreement between them, with Respect to the Time of Adjournment, he may adjourn them to such Time as he shall think proper; he shall receive Ambassadors and other public Ministers; he shall take Care that the Laws be faithfully executed, and shall Commission all the Officers of the United States.

President sole official U.S. spokesperson with other nations

About impeachment

Section 4. The President, Vice President and all civil Officers of the United States, shall be removed from Office on Impeachment for, and Conviction of, Treason, Bribery, or other high Crimes and Misdemeanors.

President can be *impeached* (accused)

Article 3: Judicial branch

Article III

Section 1. The judicial Power of the United States, shall be vested in one supreme Court, and in such inferior Courts as the Congress may from time to time ordain and establish. The Judges, both of the supreme and inferior Courts, shall hold their Offices during good Behaviour, and shall, at stated Times, receive for their Services, a Compensation, which shall not be diminished during their Continuance in Office.

Judicial power:
- hear a case
- judge a case

About *jurisdiction* of Federal courts

Section 2. The judicial Power shall extend to all Cases, in Law and Equity, arising under this Constitution, the Laws of the United States, and Treaties made, or which shall be made, under their Authority; to all Cases affecting Ambassadors, other public Ministers and Consuls; to all Cases of admiralty and maritime Jurisdiction; to Controversies to which the United States shall be a Party; to Controversies between two or more States; between a State and Citizens of another State; between Citizens of different States; between Citizens of the same State claiming Lands under Grants of different States, and between a State, or the Citizens thereof, and foreign States, Citizens or Subjects.

Changed by Amendment 11

In all Cases affecting Ambassadors, other public Ministers and Consuls, and those in which a State shall be Party, the supreme Court shall have original Jurisdiction. In all the other Cases before mentioned, the supreme Court shall have appellate Jurisdiction, both as to Law and Fact, with such Exceptions, and under such Regulations as the Congress shall make.

Guarantees a trial by jury

The Trial of all Crimes, except in Cases of Impeachment, shall be by Jury; and such Trial shall be held in the State where the said Crimes shall have been committed; but when not committed within any State, the Trial shall be at such Place or Places as the Congress may by Law have directed.

About treason

Section 3. Treason against the United States, shall consist only in levying War against them, or in adhering to their Enemies, giving them Aid and Comfort. No Person shall be convicted of Treason unless on the Testimony of two Witnesses to the same overt Act, or on Confession in open Court.

Punishes the offender *only*

The Congress shall have Power to declare the Punishment of Treason, but no Attainder of Treason shall work Corruption of Blood, or Forfeiture except during the Life of the Person attainted.

Article 4: About states

Article IV

About states' rights and duties

Section 1. Full Faith and Credit shall be given in each State to the public Acts, Records, and judicial Proceedings of every other State. And the Congress may by general Laws prescribe the Manner in which such Acts, Records and Proceedings shall be proved, and the Effect thereof.

Marriage recognized in all states

About citizens' rights and liabilities

Section 2. The Citizens of each State shall be entitled to all Privileges and Immunities of Citizens in the several States.

A Person charged in any State with Treason, Felony, or other Crime, who shall flee from Justice, and be found in another State, shall on Demand of the executive Authority of the State from which he fled, be delivered up, to be removed to the State having Jurisdiction of the Crime.

No Person held to Service or Labour in one State, under the Laws thereof, escaping into another, shall, in Consequence of any Law or Regulation therein, be discharged from such Service or Labour, but shall be delivered up on Claim of the Party to whom such Service or Labour may be due.

Outdated (about runaway slaves); see Amendment 13

About new states

Section 3. New States may be admitted by the Congress into this Union; but no new State shall be formed or erected within the Jurisdiction of any other State; nor any State be formed by the Junction of two or more States, or Parts of States, without the Consent of the Legislatures of the States concerned as well as of the Congress.

The Congress shall have Power to dispose of and make all needful Rules and Regulations respecting the Territory or other Property belonging to the United States; and nothing in this Constitution shall be so construed as to Prejudice any Claims of the United States, or of any particular State.

D.C. (District of Columbia) is *incorporated*

About guarantee to states

Section 4. The United States shall guarantee to every State in this Union a Republican Form of Government, and shall protect each of them against Invasion; and on Application of the Legislature, or of the Executive (when the Legislature cannot be convened) against domestic Violence.

Article 5:
About amendments

Article V

The Congress, whenever two thirds of both Houses shall deem it necessary, shall propose Amendments to this Constitution, or, on the Application of the Legislatures of two thirds of the several States, shall call a Convention for proposing Amendments, which, in either Case, shall be valid to all Intents and Purposes, as Part of this Constitution, when ratified by the Legislatures of three fourths of the several States, or by Conventions in three fourths thereof, as the one or the other Mode of Ratification may be proposed by the Congress; Provided that no Amendment which may be made prior to the Year One thousand eight hundred and eight shall in any Manner affect the first and fourth Clauses in the Ninth Section of the first Article; and that no State, without its Consent, shall be deprived of its equal Suffrage in the Senate.

Article 6:
About supreme law of the land

Article VI

All Debts contracted and Engagements entered into, before the Adoption of this Constitution, shall be as valid against the United States under this Constitution, as under the Confederation.

This Constitution, and the Laws of the United States which shall be made in Pursuance thereof; and all Treaties made, or which shall be made, under the Authority of the United States, shall be the supreme Law of the Land; and the Judges in every State shall be bound thereby, any Thing in the Constitution or Laws of any State to the Contrary notwithstanding.

The Senators and Representatives before mentioned, and the Members of the several State Legislatures, and all executive and judicial Officers, both of the United States and of the several States, shall be bound by Oath or Affirmation, to support this Constitution; but no religious Test shall ever be required as a Qualification to any Office or public Trust under the United States.

Article VII

The Ratification of the Conventions of nine States, shall be sufficient for the Establishment of this Constitution between the States so ratifying the Same.

• • •

Done in Convention by the Unanimous Consent of the States present the Seventeenth Day of September in the Year of our Lord one thousand seven hundred and Eighty seven and of the Independence of the United States of America the Twelfth. In witness whereof We have hereunto subscribed our Names.

G. Washington

President, and Deputy from Virginia

[Signed also by the deputies of twelve States.]

Amendments to the Constitution

The first ten
Amendments
to the
Constitution
are known as the
Bill of Rights

Amendment 1

Congress shall make no law respecting an establishment of religion, or prohibiting the free exercise thereof; or abridging the freedom of speech, or of the press; or the right of the people peaceably to assemble, and to petition the Government for a redress of grievances.

Amendment 2

A well regulated Militia, being necessary to the security of a free State, the right of the people to keep and bear Arms, shall not be infringed.

Amendment 3

No Soldier shall, in time of peace be quartered in any house, without the consent of the Owner, nor in time of war, but in a manner to be prescribed by law.

Amendment 4

The right of the people to be secure in their persons, houses, papers, and effects, against unreasonable searches and seizures, shall not be violated, and no Warrants shall issue, but upon probable cause, supported by Oath or affirmation, and particularly describing the place to be searched, and the persons or things to be seized.

Amendment 5

No person shall be held to answer for a capital, or otherwise infamous crime, unless on a presentment or indictment of a Grand Jury, except in cases arising in the land or naval forces, or in the Militia, when in actual service in time of War or public danger; nor shall any person be subject for the same offence to be twice put in jeopardy of life or limb; nor shall be compelled in any criminal case to be a witness against himself, nor be deprived of life, liberty, or property, without due process of law; nor shall private property be taken for public use, without just compensation.

Amendment 6

In all criminal prosecutions, the accused shall enjoy the right to a speedy and public trial, by an impartial jury of the State and district wherein the crime shall have been committed, which district shall have been previously ascertained by law, and to be informed of the nature and cause of the accusation; to be confronted with the witnesses against him; to have compulsory process for obtaining witnesses in his favor, and to have the Assistance of Counsel for his defense.

Amendment 7

In Suits at common law, where the value in controversy shall exceed twenty dollars, the right of trial by jury shall be preserved, and no fact tried by a jury, shall be otherwise re-examined in any Court of the United States, than according to the rules of the common law.

Amendment 8

Excessive bail shall not be required, nor excessive fines imposed, nor cruel and unusual punishments inflicted.

Amendment 9

The enumeration in the Constitution, of certain rights, shall not be construed to deny or disparage others retained by the people.

Amendment 10

The powers not delegated to the United States by the Constitution, nor prohibited by it to the States, are reserved to the States respectively, or to the people.

Amendment 11

The Judicial power of the United States shall not be construed to extend to any suit in law or equity, commenced or prosecuted against one of the United States by Citizens of another State, or by Citizens or Subjects of any Foreign State.

Amendment 12

The Electors shall meet in their respective states, and vote by ballot for President and Vice-President, one of whom, at least, shall not be an inhabitant of the same state with themselves; they shall name in their ballots the person voted for as President, and in distinct ballots the person voted for as Vice-President, and they shall make distinct lists of all persons voted for as President, and of all persons voted for as Vice-President, and of the number of votes for each, which lists they shall sign and certify, and transmit sealed to the seat of the government of the United States, directed to the President of the Senate;—The President of the Senate shall, in the presence of the Senate and House of Representatives, open all the certificates and the votes shall then be counted;—The person having the greatest number of votes for President, shall be the President, if such number be a majority of the whole number of Electors appointed; and if no person have such majority, then from the persons having the highest numbers not exceeding three on the list of those voted for as President, the House of Representatives shall choose immediately, by ballot, the President. But in choosing the President, the votes shall be taken by states, the representation from each state having one vote; a quorum for this purpose shall consist of a member or members from two-thirds of the states, and a majority of all the states shall be necessary to a choice. And if the House of Representatives shall not choose a President whenever the right of choice shall devolve upon them, before the fourth day of March next following, then the Vice-President shall act as President, as in the case of the death or other constitutional disability of the President. The person having the greatest number of votes as Vice-President, shall be the Vice-President, if such number be a majority of the whole number of Electors appointed, and if no person have a majority, then from the two highest numbers on the list, the Senate shall choose the Vice-President; a quorum for the purpose shall consist of two-thirds of the whole number of Senators, and a majority of the whole number shall be necessary to a choice. But no person constitutionally ineligible to the office of President shall be eligible to that of Vice-President of the United States.

Amendment 13

Neither slavery nor involuntary servitude, except as a punishment for crime whereof the party shall have been duly convicted, shall exist within the United States, or any place subject to their jurisdiction.

Amendment 14

Section 1. All persons born or naturalized in the United States, and subject to the jurisdiction thereof, are citizens of the United States and of the State wherein they reside. No State shall make or enforce any law which shall abridge the privileges or immunities of citizens of the United States; nor shall any State deprive any person of life, liberty, or property, without due process of law; nor deny to any person within its jurisdiction the equal protection of the laws.

Section 2. Representatives shall be apportioned among the several States according to their respective numbers, counting the whole number of persons in each State, excluding Indians not taxed. But when the right to vote at any election for the choice of electors for President and Vice President of the United States, Representatives in Congress, the Executive and Judicial officers of a State, or the members of the Legislature thereof, is denied to any of the male inhabitants of such State, being twenty-one years of age, and citizens of the United States, or in any way abridged, except for participation in rebellion, or other crime, the basis of representation therein shall be reduced in the proportion which the number of such male citizens shall bear to the whole number of male citizens twenty-one years of age in such State.

Section 3. No person shall be a Senator or Representative in Congress, or elector of President and Vice President, or hold any office, civil or military, under the United States, or under any State, who, having previously taken an oath, as a member of Congress, or as an officer of the United States, or as a member of any State legislature, or as an executive or judicial officer of any State, to support the Constitution of the United States, shall have engaged in insurrection or rebellion against the same, or given aid or comfort to the enemies thereof. But Congress may by a vote of two-thirds of each House, remove such disability.

Section 4. The validity of the public debt of the United States, authorized by law, including debts incurred for payment of pensions and bounties for services in suppressing insurrection or rebellion, shall not be questioned. But neither the United States nor any State shall assume or pay any debt or obligation incurred in aid of insurrection or rebellion against the United States, or any claim for the loss or emancipation of any slave; but all such debts, obligations and claims shall be held illegal and void.

Amendment 15

The right of citizens of the United States to vote shall not be denied or abridged by the United States or by any State on account of race, color, or previous condition of servitude.

Amendment 16

The Congress shall have power to lay and collect taxes on incomes, from whatever source derived, without apportionment among the several States, and without regard to any census or enumeration.

Amendment 17

The Senate of the United States shall be composed of two Senators from each State, elected by the people thereof, for six years; and each Senator shall have one vote. The electors in each State shall have the qualifications requisite for electors of the most numerous branch of the State legislatures.

When vacancies happen in the representation of any State in the Senate, the executive authority of such State shall issue writs of election to fill such vacancies: Provided, That the legislature of any State may empower the executive thereof to make temporary appointments until the people fill the vacancies by election as the legislature may direct.

This amendment shall not be so construed as to affect the election or term of any Senator chosen before it becomes valid as part of the Constitution.

Amendment 18

Section 1. After one year from the ratification of this article the manufacture, sale, or transportation of intoxicating liquors within, the importation thereof into, or the exportation thereof from the United States and all territory subject to the jurisdiction thereof for beverage purposes is hereby prohibited.

Section 2. The Congress and the several States shall have concurrent power to enforce this article by appropriate legislation.

Amendment 19

The right of citizens of the United States to vote shall not be denied or abridged by the United States or by any State on account of sex.

Amendment 20

Section 1. The terms of the President and Vice President shall end at noon on the 20th day of January, and the terms of Senators and Representatives at noon on the 3d day of January, of the years in which such terms would have ended if this article had not been ratified; and the terms of their successors shall then begin.

Section 2. The Congress shall assemble at least once in every year, and such meeting shall begin at noon on the 3d day of January, unless they shall by law appoint a different day.

Section 3. If, at the time fixed for the beginning of the term of the President, the President elect shall have died, the Vice President elect shall become President. If a President shall not have been chosen before the time fixed for the beginning of his term, or if the President elect shall have failed to qualify, then the Vice President elect shall act as President until a President shall have qualified; and the Congress may by law provide for the case wherein neither a President elect nor a Vice President elect shall have qualified, declaring who shall then act as President, or the manner in which one who is to act shall be selected, and such person shall act accordingly until a President or Vice President shall have qualified.

Section 4. The Congress may by law provide for the case of the death of any of the persons from whom the House of Representatives may choose a President whenever the right of choice shall have devolved upon them, and for the case of the death of any of the persons from whom the Senate may choose a Vice President whenever the right of choice shall have devolved upon them.

Amendment 21

Section 1. The eighteenth article of amendment to the Constitution of the United States is hereby repealed.

Section 2. The transportation or importation into any State, Territory, or possession of the United States for delivery or use therein of intoxicating liquors, in violation of the laws thereof, is hereby prohibited.

Amendment 22

No person shall be elected to the office of the President more than twice, and no person who has held the office of President, or acted as President, for more than two years of a term to which some other person was elected President shall be elected to the office of the President more than once. But this article shall not apply to any person holding the office of President when this article was proposed by the Congress, and shall not prevent any person who may be holding the office of President, or acting as President, during the term within which this article becomes operative from holding the office of President or acting as President during the remainder of such term.

Amendment 23

The District constituting the seat of government of the United States shall appoint in such manner as the Congress may direct:

A number of electors of President and Vice President equal to the whole number of Senators and Representatives in Congress to which the District would be entitled if it were a state, but in no event more than the least populous state; they shall be in addition to those appointed by the states, but they shall be considered, for the purposes of the election of President and Vice President, to be electors appointed by a state; and they shall meet in the District and perform such duties as provided by the twelfth article of amendment.

Amendment 24

The right of citizens of the United States to vote in any primary or other election for President or Vice President, for electors for President or Vice President, or for Senator or Representative in Congress, shall not be denied or abridged by the United States or any state by reason of failure to pay any poll tax or other tax.

Amendment 25

Section 1. In case of the removal of the President from office or of his death or resignation, the Vice President shall become President.

Section 2. Whenever there is a vacancy in the office of the Vice President, the President shall nominate a Vice President who shall take office upon confirmation by a majority vote of both Houses of Congress.

Section 3. Whenever the President transmits to the President pro tempore of the Senate and the Speaker of the House of Representatives his written declaration that he is unable to discharge the powers and duties of his office, and until he transmits to them a written declaration to the contrary, such powers and duties shall be discharged by the Vice President as Acting President.

Section 4. Whenever the Vice President and a majority of either the principal officers of the executive departments or of such other body as Congress may by law provide, transmit to the President pro tempore of the Senate and the Speaker of the House of Representatives their written declaration that the President is unable to discharge the powers and duties of his office, the Vice President shall immediately assume the powers and duties of the office as Acting President.

Thereafter, when the President transmits to the President pro tempore of the Senate and the Speaker of the House of Representatives his written declaration that no inability exists, he shall resume the powers and duties of his office unless the Vice President and a majority of either the principal officers of the executive department or of such other body as Congress may by law provide, transmit within four days to the President pro tempore of the Senate and the Speaker of the House of Representatives their written declaration that the President is unable to discharge the powers and duties of his office. Thereupon Congress shall decide the issue, assembling within forty-eight hours for that purpose if not in session. If the Congress, within twenty-one days after receipt of the latter written declaration, or, if Congress is not in session, within twenty-one days after Congress is required to assemble, determines by two-thirds vote of both Houses that the President is unable to discharge the powers and duties of his office, the Vice President shall continue to discharge the same as Acting President; otherwise, the President shall resume the powers and duties of his office.

Amendment 26

Section 1. The right of citizens of the United States, who are 18 years of age or older, to vote, shall not be denied or abridged by the United States or any state on account of age.

Section 2. The Congress shall have the power to enforce this article by appropriate legislation.

Amendment 27

No law varying the compensation for the services of the Senators and Representatives shall take effect until an election of Representatives shall have intervened.

Appéndice Cinco
Direcciones Para los Centros de Servicio del INS

La tabla siguiente contiene las direcciones del INS para que los solicitantes envíen su N-400 terminada "Solicitud Para la Naturalización." En la columna izquierda, encuentre el estado o el territorio de los E.E.U.U. donde usted vive. Lea al otro lado del estado para encontrar la dirección del Centro de Servicio del INS para su región. Esté seguro que usted envía su solicitud al Centro de Servicio señalado para su área. Si no, el trámite de la solicitud puede ser retrasado.

Si usted vive en:	Envíe su solicitud terminada a:
Arizona, California, Hawaii, Nevada, Territory of Guam, or the Commonwealth of the Northern Mariana Islands	USINS **California** Service Center Attention N-400 Unit PO Box 10400 Laguna Niguel, CA 92607-0400
Alabama, Arkansas, Florida, Georgia, Kentucky, Louisiana, Mississippi, New Mexico, North Carolina, Oklahoma, South Carolina, Tennessee, or Texas	USINS **Texas** Service Center Attention N-400 Unit PO Box 851204 Mesquite, TX 75185-1204
Alaska, Colorado, Idaho, Illinois, Indiana, Iowa, Kansas, Michigan, Minnesota, Missouri, Montana, Nebraska, North Dakota, Ohio, Oregon, South Dakota, Utah, Washington, Wisconsin, or Wyoming	USINS **Nebraska** Service Center Attention N-400 Unit PO Box 87400 Lincoln, NE 68501-7400
Connecticut, Delaware, Maine, Maryland, Massachusetts, New Hampshire, New Jersey, New York, Pennsylvania, Rhode Island, Commonwealth of Puerto Rico, U.S. Virgin Islands, Vermont, Virginia, Washington D.C., or West Virginia	USINS **Vermont** Service Center Attention N-400 Unit 75 Lower Weldon Street St Albans, VT 05479-0001

Los solicitantes en el extranjero deben enviar su solicitud al Centro de Servicio que sirve la oficina del INS en donde desean ser entrevistados. Por ejemplo, si usted quisiera que su entrevista de la naturalización fuera conducida en la oficina de Honolulu, Hawaii, entonces enviaría su solicitud al Centro de Servicio de California.

Las páginas siguientes contienen *Instrucciones del INS y una Solicitud N-400 Separable*. Observe: Rellene la solicitud *en fotocopias de plana entera de tamaño (8½" × 11")* usando las hojas separables.

Appendix Five
INS Service Center Addresses

The following table contains the INS addresses for applicants to mail their completed N-400 "Application for Naturalization." In the left column, find the state or U.S. territory were you live. Read across from your state to find the address of the INS Service Center for your region. Be certain you mail your application to the designated Service Center for your area. Otherwise, processing of your application may be delayed!

If you live in:	Send your completed application to:
Arizona, California, Hawaii, Nevada, Territory of Guam, or the Commonwealth of the Northern Mariana Islands	USINS **California** Service Center Attention N-400 Unit PO Box 10400 Laguna Niguel, CA 92607-0400
Alabama, Arkansas, Florida, Georgia, Kentucky, Louisiana, Mississippi, New Mexico, North Carolina, Oklahoma, South Carolina, Tennessee, or Texas	USINS **Texas** Service Center Attention N-400 Unit PO Box 851204 Mesquite, TX 75185-1204
Alaska, Colorado, Idaho, Illinois, Indiana, Iowa, Kansas, Michigan, Minnesota, Missouri, Montana, Nebraska, North Dakota, Ohio, Oregon, South Dakota, Utah, Washington, Wisconsin, or Wyoming	USINS **Nebraska** Service Center Attention N-400 Unit PO Box 87400 Lincoln, NE 68501-7400
Connecticut, Delaware, Maine, Maryland, Massachusetts, New Hampshire, New Jersey, New York, Pennsylvania, Rhode Island, Commonwealth of Puerto Rico, U.S. Virgin Islands, Vermont, Virginia, Washington D.C., or West Virginia	USINS **Vermont** Service Center Attention N-400 Unit 75 Lower Weldon Street St Albans, VT 05479-0001

Overseas applicants should mail their application to the Service Center that serves the INS office where they desire to be interviewed. For example, if you want your naturalization interview to be conducted at the INS office in Honolulu, Hawaii, then send your application to the California Service Center.

The next pages contain *INS Instructions* and a *Tear-Out N-400 Application*. Note: Complete your application on *full-size (8½" × 11") photocopies* of the tear-out sheets.

Importante

En las páginas siguientes proporcionamos una Solicitud N-400 para la Naturalización, así que usted puede tenerla para el uso inmediato. Sin embargo, *no cumple con los requisitos de talla de página del gobierno.*

Por lo tanto, *es absolutamente necesario fotocopiar las hojas separables usando el papel de tamaño estándar 8½″ × 11″.* Rellene su solicitud en la *fotocopia.*

Los formularios originales están disponibles del INS. Véase el Capítulo 1.

Recuerde hacer una copia de su solicitud terminada para guardar antes de enviar la original al INS.

Important

On the following pages we provide the N-400 Application for Naturalization so you may have it for immediate use. However, *it does not meet government page-size requirements.*

Therefore, *you absolutely must photocopy the tear-out sheets onto standard-size 8½″ × 11″ paper.* Complete your application on the *photocopy.*

Original forms are available from the INS. See Chapter 1.

Remember to make a copy of your completed application to keep before mailing the original to the INS.

Instructions

What Is This Form?

This form, the N-400, is an application for United States citizenship (naturalization). For more information about the naturalization process and eligibility requirements, please read *A Guide to Naturalization* (M-476). If you do not already have a copy of the *Guide*, you can get a copy from:

- the INS Web Site (www.ins.usdoj.gov);
- the National Customer Service Center (NCSC) telephone line at 1-800-375-5283 (TTY: 1-800-767-1833); or
- your local INS office.

Who Should Use This Form?

To use this form you must be at least 18 years old. You must also be **ONE** of the following:

(1) A Lawful Permanent Resident for at least 5 years;

(2) A Lawful Permanent Resident for at least 3 years
AND
- you have been married to and living with the same U.S. citizen for the last 3 years,
AND
- your spouse has been a U.S. citizen for the last 3 years;

(3) A person who has served in the U.S. Armed Forces
AND
- you are a Lawful Permanent Resident with at least 3 years of U.S. Armed Forces service **and** you are either on active duty or filing within 6 months of honorable discharge
OR
- you served during a period of recognized hostilities and enlisted or re-enlisted in the United States (you do not need to be a Lawful Permanent Resident);

(4) A member of one of several other groups who are eligible to apply for naturalization (for example, persons who are nationals but not citizens of the United States). For more information about these groups, please see the *Guide*.

Who Should NOT Use This Form?

In certain cases, a person who was born outside of the United States to U.S. citizen parents is already a citizen and does not need to apply for naturalization. To find out more information about this type of citizenship and whether you should file a Form N-600, "Application for Certificate of Citizenship," read the *Guide*.

Other permanent residents under 18 years of age may be eligible for U.S. citizenship if their U.S. citizen parent or parents file a Form N-600 application in their behalf. For more information, see "Frequently Asked Questions" in the *Guide*.

When Am I Eligible To Apply?

You may apply for naturalization when you meet **all** the requirements to become a U.S. citizen. The section of the *Guide* called "Who is Eligible for Naturalization" and the Eligibility Worksheet found in the back of the *Guide* are tools to help you determine whether you are eligible to apply for naturalization. You should complete the Worksheet before filling out this N-400 application.

If you are applying based on 5 years as a Lawful Permanent Resident or based on 3 years as a Lawful Permanent Resident married to a U.S. citizen, you may apply for naturalization up to 90 days before you meet the "continuous residence" requirement. You must meet all other requirements at the time that you file your application with us.

Certain applicants have different English and civics testing requirements based on their age and length of lawful permanent residence at the time of filing. If you are over 50 years of age and have lived in the United States as a lawful permanent resident for periods totaling at least 20 years or if you are over 55 years of age and have lived in the United States as a lawful permanent resident for periods totaling at least 15 years, you do not have to take the English test but you do have to take the civics test in the language of your choice.

If you are over 65 years of age and have lived in the United States as a lawful permanent resident for periods totaling at least 20 years, you do not have to take the English test but you do have to take a simpler version of the civics test in the language of your choice.

What Does It Cost To Apply For Naturalization and How Do I Pay?

For information on fees and form of payment, see the *Guide* insert titled "Current Naturalization Fees." Your fee is not refundable, even if you withdraw your application or it is denied.

If you are unable to pay the naturalization application fee, you may apply in writing for a fee waiver. For information about the fee waiver process, call the NCSC telephone line at 1-800-375-5283 (TTY: 1-800-767- 1833) or see the INS Web Site (www.ins.usdoj.gov) section called "Forms and Fees."

What Do I Send With My Application?

All applicants must send certain documents with their application. For information on the documents and other information you must send with your application, see the Document Checklist in the *Guide*.

Where Do I Send My Application?

You must send your N-400 application and supporting documents to an Immigration and Naturalization Service (INS) Service Center. To find the Service Center address you should use, read the section in the *Guide* called "Completing Your Application and Getting Photographed."

Applicants outside the United States who are applying on the basis of their military service should follow the instructions of their designated point of contact at a U.S. military installation.

How Do I Complete This Application?

- Please print clearly or type your answers using CAPITAL letters in each box.

- Use black or blue ink.

- **Write your INS "A"- number on the top right hand corner of each page.** Use your INS "A"- number on your Permanent Resident Card (formerly known as the Alien Registration or "Green" Card). To locate your "A"- number, see the sample Permanent Resident Cards in the *Guide*. The "A" number on your card consists of 7 to 9 numbers, depending on when your record was created. If the "A"- number on your card has fewer than 9 numbers, place enough zeros before the first number to make a *total of 9 numbers* on the application. For example, write card number A1234567 as A001234567, but write card number A12345678 as A012345678.

- If a question does not apply to you, write **N/A** (meaning "Not Applicable") in the space provided.

- If you need extra space to answer any item:
  - Attach a separate sheet of paper (or more sheets if needed);
  - Write your name, your "A"- number, and "N-400" on the top right corner of the sheet; and
  - Write the number of each question for which you are providing additional information.

Step-by-Step Instructions

This form is divided into 14 parts. The information below will help you fill out the form.

Part 1. Your Name *(the Person Applying for Naturalization)*

A. **Your current legal name -** Your current legal name is the name on your birth certificate unless it has been changed after birth by a legal action such as a marriage or court order.

B. **Your name exactly as it appears on your Permanent Resident Card** *(if different from above)*-- Write your name exactly as it appears on your card, even if it is misspelled.

C. **Other names you have used** - If you have used any other names in your life, write them in this section. If you need more space, use a separate sheet of paper.

If you have NEVER used a different name, write "N/A" in the space for "Family Name *(Last Name)."*

D. **Name change** *(optional)* - A court can allow a change in your name when you are being naturalized. A name change does not become final until a court naturalizes you. For more information regarding a name change, see the *Guide.*

If you want a court to change your name at a naturalization oath ceremony, check "Yes" and complete this section. If you do not want to change your name, check "No" and go to Part 2.

Part 2. Information About Your Eligibility

Check the box that shows why you are eligible to apply for naturalization. If the basis for your eligibility is not described in one of the first three boxes, check "Other" and briefly write the basis for your application on the lines provided.

Part 3. Information About You

A. **Social Security Number** - Print your Social Security number. If you do not have one, write "N/A" in the space provided.

B. **Date of Birth** - Always use eight numbers to show your date of birth. Write the date in this order: Month, Day, Year. For example, write May 1, 1958 as 05/01/1958.

C. **Date You Became a Permanent Resident** - Write the official date when your lawful permanent residence began, as shown on your Permanent Resident Card. To help locate the date on your card, see the sample Permanent Resident Cards in the *Guide.* Write the date in this order: Month, Day, Year. For example, write August 9, 1988 as 08/09/1988.

D. **Country of Birth** - Write the name of the country where you were born. Write the name of the country even if it no longer exists.

E. **Country of Nationality** - Write the name of the country where you are currently a citizen or national. Write the name of the country even if it no longer exists.

- If you are stateless, write the name of the country where you were last a citizen or national.

- If you are a citizen or national of more than one country, write the name of the foreign country that issued your last passport.

F. **Citizenship of Parents** - Check "Yes" if either of your parents is a U.S. citizen. If you answer "Yes," you may already be a citizen. For more information, see "Frequently Asked Questions" in the *Guide.*

G. **Current Marital Status** - Check the marital status you have on the date you are filing this application. If you are currently not married, but had a prior marriage that was annulled (declared by a court to be invalid) check "Other" and explain it.

H. **Request for Disability Waiver** - If you have a medical disability or impairment that you believe qualifies you for a waiver of the tests of English and/or U.S. government and history, check "Yes" and attach a properly completed Form N-648. If you ask for this waiver it does not guarantee that you will be excused from the testing requirements. For more information about this waiver, see the *Guide.*

I. **Request for Disability Accommodations** - We will make every reasonable effort to help applicants with disabilities complete the naturalization process. For example, if you use a wheelchair, we will make sure that you can be fingerprinted and interviewed, and can attend a naturalization ceremony at a location that is wheelchair accessible. If you are deaf or hearing impaired and need a sign language interpreter, we will make arrangements with you to have one at your interview.

If you believe you will need us to modify or change the naturalization process for you, check the box or write in the space the kind of accommodation you need. If you need more space, use a separate sheet of paper. You do not need to send us a Form N-648 to request an accommodation. You only need to send a Form N-648 to request a waiver of the test of English and/or civics.

We consider requests for accommodations on a case-by-case basis. Asking for an accommodation will not affect your eligibility for citizenship.

Part 4. Addresses and Telephone Numbers

A. **Home Address** - Give the address where you now live. Do NOT put post office (P.O.) box numbers here.

B. **Mailing Address** - If your mailing address is the same as your home address, write "same." If your mailing address is different from your home address, write it in this part.

C. **Telephone Numbers (optional)** - If you give us your telephone numbers and e-mail address, we can contact you about your application more quickly. If you are hearing impaired and use a TTY telephone connection, please indicate this by writing "(TTY)" after the telephone number.

Part 5. Information for Criminal Records Search

The Federal Bureau of Investigation (FBI) will use the information in this section, together with your fingerprints, to search for criminal records. Although the results of this search may affect your eligibility, we do NOT make naturalization decisions based on your gender, race, or physical description.

For each item, check the box that best describes you. The categories are those used by the FBI.

Part 6. Information About Your Residence and Employment

A. Write every address where you have lived during the last 5 years (including in other countries).

Begin with were you live now. Also, write the dates you lived in these places. For example, write May 1998 to June 1999 as 05/1998 to 06/1999.

If you need separate sheets of paper to complete section A or B or any other questions on this application, be sure to follow the Instructions in **"How Do I Complete This Application?"** above.

B. List where you have worked (or, if you were a student, the schools you have attended) during the last 5 years. Include military service. If you worked for yourself, write "self employed." Begin with your most recent job. Also, write the dates when you worked or studied in each place.

Part 7. Time Outside the United States *(Including Trips to Canada and Mexico and the Caribbean)*

A. Write the total number of days you spent outside of the United States (including on military service) during the last 5 years. Count the days of every trip that lasted 24 hours or longer.

B. Write the number of trips you have taken outside the United States during the last 5 years. Count every trip that lasted 24 hours or longer.

C. Provide the requested information for every trip that you have taken outside the United States since you became a Lawful Permanent Resident. Begin with your most recent trip.

Part 8. Information About Your Marital History

A. Write the number of times you have been married. Include any annulled marriages. If you were married to the same spouse more than one time, count each time as a separate marriage.

B. If you are now married, provide information about your current spouse.

C. Check the box to indicate whether your current spouse is a U.S. citizen.

D. If your spouse is a citizen through naturalization, give the date and place of naturalization. If your spouse regained U.S. citizenship, write the date and place the citizenship was regained.

E. If your spouse is not a U.S. citizen, complete this section.

F. If you were married before, give information about your former spouse or spouses. In question F.2, check the box showing the immigration status your former spouse had during your marriage. If the spouse was not a U.S. citizen or a Lawful Permanent Resident at that time check "Other" and explain. For question F.5, if your marriage was annulled, check "Other" and explain. If you were married to the same spouse more than one time, write about each marriage separately.

Note: If you or your present spouse had more than one prior marriage, provide the same information from section F and section G about every additional marriage on a separate sheet of paper.

G. For any prior marriages of your current spouse, follow the instructions in section F above.

Part 9. Information About Your Children

A. Write the total number of sons and daughters you have had. Count **all** of your children, regardless of whether they are:
- alive, missing, or dead;
- born in other countries or in the United States;
- under 18 years old or adults;
- married or unmarried;
- living with you or elsewhere;
- stepsons or stepdaughters or legally adopted; or
- born when you were not married

B. Write information about all your sons and daughters. In the last column ("Location"), write:
- "with me" - if the son or daughter is currently living with you;
- the street address and state or country where the son or daughter lives - if the son or daughter is NOT currently living with you; or

- "missing" or "dead" - if that son or daughter is missing or dead.

If you need space to list information about additional sons and daughters, attach a separate sheet of paper.

Part 10. Additional Questions

Answer each question by checking "Yes" or "No." If ANY part of a question applies to you, you must answer "Yes." For example, if you were never arrested but *were* once detained by a police officer, check "Yes" to the question "Have you ever been arrested or detained by a law enforcement officer?" and attach a written explanation.

We will use this information to determine your eligibility for citizenship. Answer every question honestly and accurately. If you do not, we may deny your application for lack of good moral character. Answering "Yes" to one of these questions does not always cause an application to be denied. For more information on eligibility, please see the *Guide*.

Part 11. Your Signature

After reading the statement in Part 11, you must sign and date it. You should sign your full name without abbreviating it or using initials. The signature must be legible. Your application may be returned to you if it is not signed.

If you cannot sign your name in English, sign in your native language. If you are unable to write in any language, sign your name with an "X."

Part 12. Signature of Person Who Prepared This Application for You

If someone filled out this form for you, he or she must complete this section.

Part 13. Signature at Interview

Do NOT complete this part. You will be asked to complete this part at your interview.

Part 14. Oath of Allegiance

Do NOT complete this part. You will be asked to complete this part at your interview.

If we approve your application, you must take this Oath of Allegiance to become a citizen. In limited cases you can take a modified Oath. The Oath requirement cannot be waived unless you are unable to understand its meaning because of a physical or developmental disability or mental impairment. For more information, see the *Guide.* Your signature on this form only indicates that you have no objections to taking the Oath of Allegiance. It does not mean that you have taken the Oath or that you are naturalized. If the INS approves your application for naturalization, you must attend an oath ceremony and take the Oath of Allegiance to the United States.

Penalties

If you knowingly and willfully falsify or conceal a material fact or submit a false document with this request, we will deny your application for naturalization and may deny any other immigration benefit. In addition, you will face severe penalties provided by law and may be subject to a removal proceeding or criminal prosecution.

If we grant you citizenship after you falsify or conceal a material fact or submit a false document with this request, your naturalization may be revoked.

Privacy Act Notice

We ask for the information on this form and for other documents to determine your eligibility for naturalization. Form N-400 processes are generally covered in 8 U.S.C. 1421 through 1430 and 1436 through 1449. We may provide information from your application to other government agencies.

Paperwork Reduction Act Notice

A person is not required to respond to a collection of information unless it displays a valid OMB control number. We try to create forms and instructions that are accurate, can be easily understood and which impose the least possible burden on you to provide us with the information. Often this is difficult because some immigration laws are very complex. The estimated average time to complete and file this form is computed as follows: (1) 2 hours and 8 minutes to learn about and complete the form; (2) 4 hours to assemble and file the information - for a total estimated average of 6 hours and 8 minutes per application. If you have comments about the accuracy of this estimate or suggestions to make this form simpler, you can write to the Immigration and Naturalization Service, HQPDI, 425 I Street, N.W., Room 4307r, Washington, DC 20536; OMB No. 1115-0009. **DO NOT MAIL YOUR COMPLETED APPLICATION TO THIS ADDRESS.**

Print clearly or type your answers using CAPITAL letters. Failure to print clearly may delay your application. Use black or blue ink.

Part 1. Your Name *(The Person Applying for Naturalization)*

Write your INS "A"- number here:

A _ _ _ _ _ _ _ _ _

A. Your current legal name.

Family Name *(Last Name)*

FOR INS USE ONLY

Given Name *(First Name)*

Full Middle Name *(If applicable)*

Bar Code	Date Stamp

B. Your name <u>exactly</u> as it appears on your Permanent Resident Card.

Family Name *(Last Name)*

Given Name *(First Name)*

Full Middle Name *(If applicable)*

Remarks

C. If you have ever used other names, provide them below.

Family Name *(Last Name)*	Given Name *(First Name)*	Middle Name

D. Name change *(optional)*

Please read the Instructions before you decide whether to change your name.

1. Would you like to legally change your name? ☐ Yes ☐ No

2. If "Yes," print the new name you would like to use. Do not use initials or abbreviations when writing your new name.

Family Name *(Last Name)*

Given Name *(First Name)*

Full Middle Name

Action

Part 2. Information About Your Eligibility *(Check Only One)*

I am at least 18 years old **AND**

A. ☐ I have been a Lawful Permanent Resident of the United States for at least 5 years.

B. ☐ I have been a Lawful Permanent Resident of the United States for at least 3 years, AND I have been married to and living with the same U.S. citizen for the last 3 years, AND my spouse has been a U.S. citizen for the last 3 years.

C. ☐ I am applying on the basis of qualifying military service.

D. ☐ Other *(Please explain)* _____

Part 3. Information About You

Write your INS "A"- number here:

A __ __ __ __ __ __ __ __ __

A. Social Security Number

___ ___ ___ - ___ ___ - ___ ___ ___ ___

B. Date of Birth *(Month/Day/Year)*

___ ___ / ___ ___ / ___ ___ ___ ___

C. Date You Became a Permanent Resident *(Month/Day/Year)*

___ ___ ___ ___ ___ ___ ___ ___

D. Country of Birth

E. Country of Nationality

F. Are either of your parents U.S. citizens? *(if yes, see Instructions)* ☐ Yes ☐ No

G. What is your current marital status? ☐ Single, Never Married ☐ Married ☐ Divorced ☐ Widowed

☐ Marriage Annulled or Other *(Explain)* _____

H. Are you requesting a waiver of the English and/or U.S. History and Government requirements based on a disability or impairment and attaching a Form N-648 with your application? ☐ Yes ☐ No

I. Are you requesting an accommodation to the naturalization process because of a disability or impairment? *(See Instructions for some examples of accommodations.)* ☐ Yes ☐ No

If you answered "Yes", check the box below that applies:

☐ I am deaf or hearing impaired and need a sign language interpreter who uses the following language: _____

☐ I use a wheelchair.

☐ I am blind or sight impaired.

☐ I will need another type of accommodation. Please explain: _____

_____

_____

Part 4. Addresses and Telephone Numbers

A. Home Address - Street Number and Name *(Do NOT write a P.O. Box in this space)*

Apartment Number

City	County	State	ZIP Code	Country

B. Care of

Mailing Address - Street Number and Name *(If different from home address)*

Apartment Number

City	State	ZIP Code	Country

C. Daytime Phone Number *(If any)*

( )

Evening Phone Number *(If any)*

( )

E-mail Address *(If any)*

Note: The categories below are those required by the FBI. See Instructions for more information.

A. Gender

☐ Male ☐ Female

B. Height

| Feet | Inches |

C. Weight

| Pounds |

D. Race

☐ White ☐ Asian or Pacific Islander ☐ Black ☐ American Indian or Alaskan Native ☐ Unknown

E. Hair color

☐ Black ☐ Brown ☐ Blonde ☐ Gray ☐ White ☐ Red ☐ Sandy ☐ Bald (No Hair)

F. Eye color

☐ Brown ☐ Blue ☐ Green ☐ Hazel ☐ Gray ☐ Black ☐ Pink ☐ Maroon ☐ Other

Part 6. Information About Your Residence and Employment

A. Where have you lived during the last 5 years? Begin with where you live now and then list every place you lived for the last 5 years. If you need more space, use a separate sheet of paper.

Street Number and Name, Apartment Number, City, State, Zip Code and Country	Dates (Month/Year)	
	From	To
Current Home Address - Same as Part 4.A	_ _/_ _ _ _	Present
	_ _/_ _ _ _	_ _ _ _ _
	_ _/_ _ _ _	_ _ _ _ _
	_ _/_ _ _ _	_ _ _ _ _
	_ _/_ _ _ _	_ _ _ _ _

B. Where have you worked (or, if you were a student, what schools did you attend) during the last 5 years? Include military service. Begin with your current or latest employer and then list every place you have worked or studied for the last 5 years. If you need more space, use a separate sheet of paper.

Employer or School Name	Employer or School Address (Street, City and State)	Dates (Month/Year)		Your Occupation
		From	To	
		_ _/_ _ _ _	_ _/_ _ _ _	
		_ _/_ _ _ _	_ _/_ _ _ _	
		_ _/_ _ _ _	_ _/_ _ _ _	
		_ _/_ _ _ _	_ _/_ _ _ _	
		_ _/_ _ _ _	_ _/_ _ _ _	

Write your INS "A"- number here:

A _ _ _ _ _ _ _ _ _ _ _

A. How many total days did you spend outside of the United States during the past 5 years?

[   ] days

B. How many trips of 24 hours or more have you taken outside of the United States during the past 5 years?

[   ] trips

C. List below all the trips of 24 hours or more that you have taken outside of the United States since becoming a Lawful
Permanent Resident. Begin with your most recent trip. If you need more space, use a separate sheet of paper.

Date You Left the United States *(Month/Day/Year)*	Date You Returned to the United States *(Month/Day/Year)*	Did Trip Last 6 Months or More?	Countries to Which You Traveled	Total Days Out of the United States
__/__/____	__/__/____	☐ Yes ☐ No		
__/__/____	__/__/____	☐ Yes ☐ No		
__/__/____	__/__/____	☐ Yes ☐ No		
__/__/____	__/__/____	☐ Yes ☐ No		
__/__/____	__/__/____	☐ Yes ☐ No		
__/__/____	__/__/____	☐ Yes ☐ No		
__/__/____	__/__/____	☐ Yes ☐ No		
__/__/____	__/__/____	☐ Yes ☐ No		
__/__/____	__/__/____	☐ Yes ☐ No		
__/__/____	__/__/____	☐ Yes ☐ No		

A. How many times have you been married (including annulled marriages)? [   ] If you have NEVER been married, go to Part 9.

B. If you are now married, give the following information about your spouse:

1. Spouse's Family Name *(Last Name)*   Given Name *(First Name)*   Full Middle Name *(If applicable)*

[   ] [   ] [   ]

2. Date of Birth *(Month/Day/Year)*   3. Date of Marriage *(Month/Day/Year)*   4. Spouse's Social Security Number

___/__/____   ___/__/____   ___-__-____

5. Home Address - Street Number and Name   Apartment Number

[   ] [   ]

City   State   ZIP Code

[   ] [   ] [   ]

Part 8. Information About Your Marital History (Continued)

C. Is your spouse a U.S. citizen? ☐ Yes ☐ No

D. If your spouse is a U.S. citizen, give the following information:

1. When did your spouse become a U.S. citizen? ☐ At Birth ☐ Other

   If "Other," give the following information:

2. Date your spouse became a U.S. citizen

   ___/___/_____

3. Place your spouse became a U.S. citizen *(Please see Instructions)*

   City and State

E. If your spouse is NOT a U.S. citizen, give the following information :

1. Spouse's Country of Citizenship

2. Spouse's INS "A"- Number *(If applicable)*

   A_ _ _ _ _ _ _ _ _

3. Spouse's Immigration Status

   ☐ Lawful Permanent Resident ☐ Other _____

F. If you were married before, provide the following information about your prior spouse. If you have more than one previous marriage, use a separate sheet of paper to provide the information requested in questions 1-5 below.

1. Prior Spouse's Family Name *(Last Name)*　Given Name *(First Name)*　Full Middle Name *(If applicable)*

2. Prior Spouse's Immigration Status

   ☐ U.S. Citizen

   ☐ Lawful Permanent Resident

   ☐ Other _____

3. Date of Marriage *(Month/Day/Year)*

   ___/___/_____

4. Date Marriage Ended *(Month/Day/Year)*

   ___/___/_____

5. How Marriage Ended

   ☐ Divorce ☐ Spouse Died ☐ Other _____

G. How many times has your current spouse been married (including annulled marriages)? ☐

   If your spouse has EVER been married before, give the following information about your spouse's prior marriage.
   If your spouse has more than one previous marriage, use a separate sheet of paper to provide the information requested in questions
   1 - 5 below.

1. Prior Spouse's Family Name *(Last Name)*　Given Name *(First Name)*　Full Middle Name *(If applicable)*

2. Prior Spouse's Immigration Status

   ☐ U.S. Citizen

   ☐ Lawful Permanent Resident

   ☐ Other _____

3. Date of Marriage *(Month/Day/Year)*

   ___/___/_____

4. Date Marriage Ended *(Month/Day/Year)*

   ___/___/_____

5. How Marriage Ended

   ☐ Divorce ☐ Spouse Died ☐ Other _____

A. How many sons and daughters have you had? For more information on which sons and daughters you should include and how to complete this section, see the Instructions.

B. Provide the following information about all of your sons and daughters. If you need more space, use a separate sheet of paper.

Full Name of Son or Daughter	Date of Birth (Month/Day/Year)	INS "A"- number (if child has one)	Country of Birth	Current Address (Street, City, State & Country)
	__ __/__ __/__ __ __ __	A__ __ __ __ __ __ __ __ __		
	__ __/__ __/__ __ __ __	A__ __ __ __ __ __ __ __ __		
	__ __/__ __/__ __ __ __	A__ __ __ __ __ __ __ __ __		
	__ __/__ __/__ __ __ __	A__ __ __ __ __ __ __ __ __		
	__ __/__ __/__ __ __ __	A__ __ __ __ __ __ __ __ __		
	__ __/__ __/__ __ __ __	A__ __ __ __ __ __ __ __ __		
	__ __/__ __/__ __ __ __	A__ __ __ __ __ __ __ __ __		
	__ __/__ __/__ __ __ __	A__ __ __ __ __ __ __ __ __		

Part 10. Additional Questions

Please answer questions 1 through 14. If you answer "Yes" to any of these questions, include a written explanation with this form. Your written explanation should (1) explain why your answer was "Yes," and (2) provide any additional information that helps to explain your answer.

A. General Questions

1. Have you **EVER** claimed to be a U.S. citizen *(in writing or any other way)*? ☐ Yes ☐ No

2. Have you **EVER** registered to vote in any Federal, state, or local election in the United States? ☐ Yes ☐ No

3. Have you **EVER** voted in any Federal, state, or local election in the United States? ☐ Yes ☐ No

4. Since becoming a Lawful Permanent Resident, have you **EVER** failed to file a required Federal, state, or local tax return? ☐ Yes ☐ No

5. Do you owe any Federal, state, or local taxes that are overdue? ☐ Yes ☐ No

6. Do you have any title of nobility in any foreign country? ☐ Yes ☐ No

7. Have you ever been declared legally incompetent or been confined to a mental institution within the last 5 years? ☐ Yes ☐ No

B. Affiliations

8. a. Have you **EVER** been a member of or associated with any organization, association, fund, foundation, party, club, society, or similar group in the United States or in any other place? ☐ Yes ☐ No

b. If you answered "Yes," list the name of each group below. If you need more space, attach the names of the other group(s) on a separate sheet of paper.

Name of Group	Name of Group
1.	6.
2.	7.
3.	8.
4.	9.
5.	10.

9. Have you **EVER** been a member of or in any way associated *(either directly or indirectly)* with:

   a. The Communist Party? ☐ Yes ☐ No

   b. Any other totalitarian party? ☐ Yes ☐ No

   c. A terrorist organization? ☐ Yes ☐ No

10. Have you **EVER** advocated *(either directly or indirectly)* the overthrow of any government by force or violence? ☐ Yes ☐ No

11. Have you **EVER** persecuted *(either directly or indirectly)* any person because of race, religion, national origin, membership in a particular social group, or political opinion? ☐ Yes ☐ No

12. Between March 23, 1933, and May 8, 1945, did you work for or associate in any way *(either directly or indirectly)* with:

   a. The Nazi government of Germany? ☐ Yes ☐ No

   b. Any government in any area (1) occupied by, (2) allied with, or (3) established with the help of the Nazi government of Germany? ☐ Yes ☐ No

   c. Any German, Nazi, or S.S. military unit, paramilitary unit, self-defense unit, vigilante unit, citizen unit, police unit, government agency or office, extermination camp, concentration camp, prisoner of war camp, prison, labor camp, or transit camp? ☐ Yes ☐ No

C. Continuous Residence

Since becoming a Lawful Permanent Resident of the United States:

13. Have you **EVER** called yourself a "nonresident" on a Federal, state, or local tax return? ☐ Yes ☐ No

14. Have you **EVER** failed to file a Federal, state, or local tax return because you considered yourself to be a "nonresident"? ☐ Yes ☐ No

Write your INS "A"- number here:

A _ _ _ _ _ _ _ _ _

D. Good Moral Character

For the purposes of this application, you must answer "Yes" to the following questions, if applicable, even if your records were sealed or otherwise cleared or if anyone, including a judge, law enforcement officer, or attorney, told you that you no longer have a record.

15. Have you **EVER** committed a crime or offense for which you were NOT arrested? ☐ Yes ☐ No

16. Have you **EVER** been arrested, cited, or detained by any law enforcement officer (including INS and military officers) for any reason? ☐ Yes ☐ No

17. Have you **EVER** been charged with committing any crime or offense? ☐ Yes ☐ No

18. Have you **EVER** been convicted of a crime or offense? ☐ Yes ☐ No

19. Have you **EVER** been placed in an alternative sentencing or a rehabilitative program (for example: diversion, deferred prosecution, withheld adjudication, deferred adjudication)? ☐ Yes ☐ No

20. Have you **EVER** received a suspended sentence, been placed on probation, or been paroled? ☐ Yes ☐ No

21. Have you **EVER** been in jail or prison? ☐ Yes ☐ No

If you answered "Yes" to any of questions 15 through 21, complete the following table. If you need more space, use a separate sheet of paper to give the same information.

Why were you arrested, cited, detained, or charged?	Date arrested, cited, detained, or charged *(Month/Day/Year)*	Where were you arrested, cited, detained or charged? *(City, State, Country)*	Outcome or disposition of the arrest, citation, detention or charge *(No charges filed, charges dismissed, jail, probation, etc.)*

Answer questions 22 through 33. If you answer "Yes" to any of these questions, attach (1) your written explanation why your answer was "Yes," and (2) any additional information or documentation that helps explain your answer.

22. Have you **EVER:**

    a. been a habitual drunkard? ☐ Yes ☐ No

    b. been a prostitute, or procured anyone for prostitution? ☐ Yes ☐ No

    c. sold or smuggled controlled substances, illegal drugs or narcotics? ☐ Yes ☐ No

    d. been married to more than one person at the same time? ☐ Yes ☐ No

    e. helped anyone enter or try to enter the United States illegally? ☐ Yes ☐ No

    f. gambled illegally or received income from illegal gambling? ☐ Yes ☐ No

    g. failed to support your dependents or to pay alimony? ☐ Yes ☐ No

23. Have you **EVER** given false or misleading information to any U.S. government official while applying for any immigration benefit or to prevent deportation, exclusion, or removal? ☐ Yes ☐ No

24. Have you **EVER** lied to any U.S. government official to gain entry or admission into the United States? ☐ Yes ☐ No

E. Removal, Exclusion, and Deportation Proceedings

25. Are removal, exclusion, rescission or deportation proceedings pending against you? ☐ Yes ☐ No

26. Have you **EVER** been removed, excluded, or deported from the United States? ☐ Yes ☐ No

27. Have you **EVER** been ordered to be removed, excluded, or deported from the United States? ☐ Yes ☐ No

28. Have you **EVER** applied for any kind of relief from removal, exclusion, or deportation? ☐ Yes ☐ No

F. Military Service

29. Have you **EVER** served in the U.S. Armed Forces? ☐ Yes ☐ No

30. Have you **EVER** left the United States to avoid being drafted into the U.S. Armed Forces? ☐ Yes ☐ No

31. Have you **EVER** applied for any kind of exemption from military service in the U.S. Armed Forces? ☐ Yes ☐ No

32. Have you **EVER** deserted from the U.S. Armed Forces? ☐ Yes ☐ No

G. Selective Service Registration

33. Are you a male who lived in the United States at any time between your 18th and 26th birthdays in any status except as a lawful nonimmigrant? ☐ Yes ☐ No

If you answered "NO", go on to question 34.

If you answered "YES", provide the information below.

If you answered "YES", but you did NOT register with the Selective Service System and are still under 26 years of age, you must register before you apply for naturalization, so that you can complete the information below:

Date Registered (Month/Day/Year) [   ]   Selective Service Number [_ _ / _ _ _ / _ _ _ _]

If you answered "YES", but you did NOT register with the Selective Service and you are now 26 years old or older, attach a statement explaining why you did not register.

H. Oath Requirements *(See Part 14 for the text of the oath)*

Answer questions 34 through 39. If you answer "No" to any of these questions, attach (1) your written explanation why the answer was "No" and (2) any additional information or documentation that helps to explain your answer.

34. Do you support the Constitution and form of government of the United States? ☐ Yes ☐ No

35. Do you understand the full Oath of Allegiance to the United States? ☐ Yes ☐ No

36. Are you willing to take the full Oath of Allegiance to the United States? ☐ Yes ☐ No

37. If the law requires it, are you willing to bear arms on behalf of the United States? ☐ Yes ☐ No

38. If the law requires it, are you willing to perform noncombatant services in the U.S. Armed Forces? ☐ Yes ☐ No

39. If the law requires it, are you willing to perform work of national importance under civilian direction? ☐ Yes ☐ No

Part 11. Your Signature

Write your INS "A"- number here:

A _ _ _ _ _ _ _ _ _

I certify, under penalty of perjury under the laws of the United States of America, that this application, and the evidence submitted with it, are all true and correct. I authorize the release of any information which INS needs to determine my eligibility for naturalization.

Your Signature

Date *(Month/Day/Year)*

___/___/_____

Part 12. Signature of Person Who Prepared This Application for You *(if applicable)*

I declare under penalty of perjury that I prepared this application at the request of the above person. The answers provided are based on information of which I have personal knowledge and/or were provided to me by the above named person in response to the *exact questions* contained on this form.

Preparer's Printed Name

Preparer's Signature

Date *(Month/Day/Year)*

___/___/_____

Preparer's Firm or Organization Name *(If applicable)*

Preparer's Daytime Phone Number

(   )

Preparer's Address - Street Number and Name

City

State

ZIP Code

Do Not Complete Parts 13 and 14 Until an INS Officer Instructs You To Do So

Part 13. Signature at Interview

I swear (affirm) and certify under penalty of perjury under the laws of the United States of America that I know that the contents of this application for naturalization subscribed by me, including corrections numbered 1 through ____ and the evidence submitted by me numbered pages 1 through ____, are true and correct to the best of my knowledge and belief.

Subscribed to and sworn to (affirmed) before me

Officer's Printed Name or Stamp

Date *(Month/Day/Year)*

Complete Signature of Applicant

Officer's Signature

Part 14. Oath of Allegiance

If your application is approved, you will be scheduled for a public oath ceremony at which time you will be required to take the following oath of allegiance immediately prior to becoming a naturalized citizen. By signing below, you acknowledge your willingness and ability to take this oath:

I hereby declare, on oath, that I absolutely and entirely renounce and abjure all allegiance and fidelity to any foreign prince, potentate, state, or sovereignty, of whom or which which I have heretofore been a subject or citizen;

that I will support and defend the Constitution and laws of the United States of America against all enemies, foreign and domestic;
that I will bear true faith and allegiance to the same;
that I will bear arms on behalf of the United States when required by the law;
that I will perform noncombatant service in the Armed Forces of the United States when required by the law;
that I will perform work of national importance under civilian direction when required by the law; and
that I take this obligation freely, without any mental reservation or purpose of evasion; so help me God.

Printed Name of Applicant

Complete Signature of Applicant

_____

Applicant's Name

A _ _ _ _ _ _ _ _ _

Permanent Resident #

Part Number	Section	Explanation

Part Number	Section	Explanation

Part Number	Section	Explanation

U.S. Department of Justice
Immigration and Naturalization Service

Important Document Information

The Immigration and Naturalization Service has changed the policy requiring submission of original documents or certified copies of documents with applications and petitions.

You may now submit ordinary legible photocopies of the original documents required, including Naturalization Certificates and Alien Registration Cards. Please submit copies of both sides of documents. You may be required to present the original documents during any subsequent contacts with the Service.

The following statement must be signed and dated by either the applicant, the petitioner, or the attorney, *and submitted with each petition and/or application.*

"Copies of documents submitted are exact photocopies of unaltered original documents and I understand that I may be required to submit original documents to an Immigration or Consular official at a later date."

Signature: _____

Typed or Printed Name: _____

Date: _____

FC-023
01/19/00